SEA
FISHING
DISASTERS

SEA FISHING DISASTERS

CHRISTOPHER MIDDLETON

PEN & SWORD
MARITIME

First published in Great Britain in 2025 by
PEN AND SWORD MARITIME
an imprint of
Pen and Sword Books Ltd
Yorkshire – Philadelphia

Typeset in Times New Roman 12/16 by
SJmagic DESIGN SERVICES, India.
Printed and bound in the UK by CPI Group (UK) Ltd.

The Publisher's authorised representative in the EU for product safety is Authorised Rep
Compliance Ltd., Ground Floor, 71 Lower Baggot Street, Dublin D02 P593, Ireland.
www.arccompliance.com

For a complete list of Pen & Sword titles please contact
PEN & SWORD BOOKS LIMITED
George House, Units 12 & 13, Beevor Street, Off Pontefract Road,
Barnsley, South Yorkshire, S71 1HN, England
E-mail: enquiries@pen-and-sword.co.uk
Website: www.pen-and-sword.co.uk

or
PEN AND SWORD BOOKS
1950 Lawrence Rd, Havertown, PA 19083, USA
E-mail: uspen-and-sword@casematepublishers.com
Website: www.penandswordbooks.com

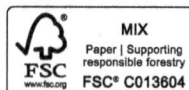

MIX
Paper | Supporting
responsible forestry
FSC
www.fsc.org   FSC® C013604

Contents

Introduction vi

Chapter 1   FV *Gaul* 1

Chapter 2   The Eyemouth Fishing Disaster 15

Chapter 3   *Ehime Maru* and USS *Greeneville* Collision 21

Chapter 4   The *Bugaled Breizh* 33

Chapter 5   The *Pelican* 50

Chapter 6   The Morecambe Bay Cockling Disaster 66

Chapter 7   FV *Antares* 78

Chapter 8   *Solway Harvester* 90

Chapter 9   The 1914 Newfoundland Sealing Disasters 111

Chapter 10   FV *Destination* 137

Chapter 11   José Salvador Alvarenga 154

Chapter 12   The Seaham Lifeboat Disaster 169

Bibliography 178

Introduction

Commercial fishing is the most dangerous peacetime occupation in Britain, with the death rate among commercial fishermen being 115 times higher than the general UK workforce. This book looks at some of the most well-known disasters which have taken place within the commercial fishing industry, covering incidents both in Britain and across the world.

Sea Fishing Disasters consists of twelve chapters, each focusing on a different sea fishing disaster. These range from the Eyemouth Fishing Disaster which took place in the 1800s, to those in the twenty-first century, such as the loss of the *Solway Harvester* and FV *Destination*. Several different types of fishing disasters are examined with incidents involving trawlers, dredgers, shellfish pickers, seal hunters and recreational anglers all being covered.

Chapter 1

FV *Gaul*

FV *Gaul* was a British deep sea trawler which was lost after having been caught in a storm in the Barents Sea off the northern coast of Norway on 8 February 1974. No distress call was issued and the entire crew of thirty-six men lost their lives. The British government's reluctance to search for the wreck of the *Gaul*, and the fact that the vessel was lost at the peak of the Cold War, led many to believe that the true reason for the sinking of the *Gaul* was being concealed. Today, a clearer picture of what happened to the *Gaul* exists, but many questions remain over the role of the vessel and the government's response to its loss.

The *Gaul* was built by Brooke Marine in Lowestoft, Suffolk, for the Ranger Fishing company of North Shields, Tyneside. It was the final ship of a class of four built for Ranger Fishing and was originally named the *Ranger Castor*. At 66 metres (216 ft) in length, and with a tonnage of 1,106, the *Gaul* was a large factory fishing vessel which was able to stay out at sea for weeks at a time and could process, freeze and store over 350 tons of fish and 120 tons of fishmeal.

The *Ranger Castor* was launched in December 1971 and was delivered to Ranger Fishing in the summer of 1972. In 1973, British United Trawlers bought the *Ranger Castor*. It was renamed FV *Gaul* and relocated to Hull, where the company was based.

The Last Voyage of the *Gaul*

In January 1974, the *Gaul* departed St Andrew's Dock in Hull headed to the Barents Sea between the northern coast of Norway and Russia's Novaya Zemlya archipelago. During the journey, the mate, George Petty, began to feel ill. He could not continue and was taken to a port on the Norwegian island of Lødingen where he left the ship. Two days later, the *Gaul* sailed to Tromsø, where Maurice Spurgeon joined the ship, bringing the crew back up to its full complement of thirty-six. The *Gaul* then sailed to the Barents Sea, where it joined several other British fishing vessels, including two of its sister ships.

For around a week, the *Gaul* fished in calm weather with no incidents or complications arising, but by the early hours of 8 February, the weather conditions began to deteriorate. The crew of the *Gaul* lost sight of the other vessels they had been fishing alongside and were forced to "lay and dodge" – turn to face into the waves and wind bow on, which was the standard procedure during bad weather and rough seas. By late morning, the *Gaul* was at the Northern Cape Bank area of the Barents Sea, and conditions had worsened. The Marine Accident Investigation Branch (MAIB) report into the incident (which was published in 1999) said that the skippers of other vessels operating nearby "reported that conditions that day were as bad as they had ever experienced." It was estimated that the storm the *Gaul* was in the middle of would have been rated 10 on the Beaufort Scale, meaning windspeeds of 55 knots (63 mph) and waves up to 12.5 metres (41 ft) high.

By 9 February, the *Gaul* had yet to make radio contact with any other fishing boats or shore establishments. Initially, this was not a cause for concern as no distress signal or mayday call had been issued by the *Gaul*. But by the morning of 10 February, radio contact had still not been made, the alarm was raised, and the search for the *Gaul* began.

Over twenty British and Norwegian trawlers operating in the area stopped fishing and began to search for the *Gaul*. They were joined by the Royal Navy aircraft carrier HMS *Hermes*, the frigate HMS *Mohawk*, and vessels from the Royal Norwegian Navy. Royal Norwegian Air Force Orion patrol aircraft were launched from Andøya Air Station and made thirteen sorties to search for the *Gaul*, while RAF Nimrod aircraft searched four areas of the Barents Sea and Sea King helicopters and Norwegian coastguard cutters searched the coastline of Norway. Despite 285,000 square kilometres (177,000 sq. miles) of sea being searched, no sign of the *Gaul*, its lifeboat or its inflatable life rafts could be found. After five days, the search was called off, although lower-intensity searches continued for several further weeks. It was not until three months later that the first confirmed sign of the *Gaul* was located when a Norwegian merchant vessel recovered a lifebuoy stamped with the words *GAUL*, HULL.

The Initial Investigation

Investigations soon began to try and work out exactly what had happened. The first of which was carried out in late 1974 under the Merchant Shipping Act and concluded that the *Gaul* was likely to have sunk when it was overwhelmed by enormous waves and heavy seas during the storm. The crew's families were highly dissatisfied with this conclusion, as were other commercial fishermen and marine shipping experts. They stated that the *Gaul* was specifically designed to withstand such conditions and had ample safety equipment, being fitted with a lifeboat, six inflatable life rafts and more lifejackets than there were crewmembers on board. While the storm of 8 February was severe, they pointed out that the *Gaul*'s two sister ships endured similar conditions and survived with no major issues encountered, and even if the *Gaul* had found itself in difficulties, it would almost certainly have had time to issue a distress call.

The British government refused to conduct further searches for the *Gaul*, stating that locating the wreck would be too dangerous, expensive and time-consuming. They also claimed that there were a vast number of wrecks from the Arctic convoys of the Second World War in the Barents Sea and distinguishing between them and the *Gaul* would be almost impossible and, even if the wreck of the *Gaul* was located, it would not necessarily mean the reason for its sinking could be established. This reluctance to search for the *Gaul* was heavily criticised by both the crew's families and the media and led to accusations that the British government was deliberately trying to conceal what had happened.

Conspiracy Theories

With no wreck to examine, a wide range of speculative theories were put forward to explain the loss of the vessel. These included the *Gaul* capsizing due to excessive ice build-up on its superstructure and the *Gaul* sinking due to damage received in a collision with another ship. But many explanations revolved around the *Gaul* coming into conflict with the Soviet Navy. Claims at the time speculated that the *Gaul* may have been being used as a spy ship, with its crew given equipment by the Royal Navy or British intelligence services to track and report on the movement of Soviet ships. If this was true, then it may have been the case that the Soviet Navy became aware of the *Gaul*'s actions and attacked the ship with torpedoes or missiles, or boarded the *Gaul* and arrested the crew. Other theories put forward the idea that the *Gaul* sank when it was dragged underwater when nets became tangled on a submerged submarine; it struck a mine; or that it collided with a British destroyer or frigate; or was rammed by a Soviet warship and became so damaged that it then sank in the storm. It was also claimed that the *Gaul* could have sunk due to its trawl nets becoming snagged on SOSUS (Sound Surveillance System) cables. These cables linked a series of underwater hydrophones used by the US military to listen to Soviet submarines and track their movements. While the existence of SOSUS cables was known, their exact location remained classified until the 1990s, leading to speculation that the true reason for the loss of the *Gaul* could not be revealed without the details of SOSUS becoming known to the Russians.

Despite marine experts who specialised in the recovery of wrecked ships insisting that the wreck of the *Gaul* would be relatively easy to locate, the British government still refused to initiate searches for the vessel, allowing the rumours, speculation and conspiracy theories to continue to grow. The families of the crew were distraught at the lack of action being taken to locate the vessel, with many becoming certain that the government had ulterior motives for refusing to search for the wreck. The spy ship claims added to their distress, especially as it left open the agonizing possibility that the crew had not died when the vessel sank but had instead been captured and were still alive and being held in captivity somewhere within the Soviet Union. The British government strongly denied the spy ship claims, maintaining that trawler crews were never used to track the movements of Soviet vessels, and that Royal Navy personnel were never placed on fishing boats to carry out the same role.

But in July 1974, five months after the loss of the *Gaul*, John Prescott, the Member of Parliament for Kingston upon Hull East, wrote to the Ministry of Defence asking if Royal Navy personnel were deployed on trawlers. He received a reply from Mr Frank Judd, the Parliamentary Under Secretary of State of Defence, stating that Royal Navy personnel did "embark in trawlers from time to time" and that it was "by no means unusual for junior officers to spend some time on board trawlers to gain sea-going experience." This led to stories in the *Guardian* and *Daily Mail* that the *Gaul* was indeed being used as a spy ship and added credibility to the claims that the Soviet Navy targeted the *Gaul*.

MPs from Hull and the surrounding areas wrote letters to the government, imploring them to fully explain the links between the Royal Navy and the British trawler fleet. Bill Rodgers, the Minister of State for Defence, wrote to fellow MPs and the family members of the *Gaul*'s crew in August 1974. The letter reiterated that Royal Navy personnel were placed on trawlers to gain seagoing experience and went on to say that he could "categorically assure" them that "no RN personnel or MOD equipment were on board *Gaul*" and that British trawlers did not take part in intelligence gathering on behalf of the government

This did little to quell the speculation and many families believed that the government would not restart the search because the *Gaul* had been sunk by Soviet warships and the discovery of the wreck would prove this. The spy ship claims also led to entirely unsubstantiated claims that other fishing vessels had seen the *Gaul* being escorted toward the Russian coastline by Soviet warships and that a distress call had been sent by the *Gaul* and received by a Danish radio station but, after coming under pressure from the British government, the radio station was forced to deny this.

The Lifebuoy, Crew Member Sightings and Refusal to Search for the Wreck

In 1975, two episodes of the ITV current affairs programme *This Week* were broadcast which centred on the *Gaul* and the theories and suspicions surrounding its loss. This brought the *Gaul* to a broader audience and once again increased the speculation and rumours over the vessel's fate. It was also claimed that the lifebuoy from the *Gaul* – the only physical evidence which had been found – was too clean and lacking in marine vegetation to have been at sea for three months, meaning that it must have been planted in the area in an attempt to create the impression that the *Gaul* had been lost at sea. This proved to be a controversial issue, with a microbiologist named Mr Hendey, who examined the lifebuoy, stating in the first official investigation that there was an "absence of deep water plankton" present on the lifebuoy and that traces of a freshwater species of algae could also be found on its surface. He concluded that this meant that the lifebuoy had not been submerged in deep saltwater for a significant amount of time and was likely to have only briefly floated in shallow water.

In 1982, rumours emerged that John Doone, the *Gaul*'s radio operator, had been seen alive in a pub in Port Elizabeth, South Africa, four years after the *Gaul* was lost. A man named Alan Waterworth, who had previously been a work colleague of Doone, was quoted in the press at the time as saying "As far as I am concerned it was him ... that was John Doone." This started a search for John Doone throughout the 1980s and 1990s.

While he was never found, this added to the belief that the official story of the loss of the *Gaul* was untrue and fuelled further conspiracy theories.

In late 1975, the Norwegian trawler *Rairo* reported snagging its nets on a previously unknown underwater obstruction in the Northern Cape Bank area of the Barents Sea. This was consistent with the last known location of the *Gaul* and heavily suggested that the *Rairo* had inadvertently found the wreck. In 1977, another trawler, *Coriolanus*, found the wreck of a vessel on its echo sounder in the same location where the *Rairo* had snagged its nets. The British government refused to act on these new developments.

Indeed, until the early 1990s, the British government maintained its belief that finding the *Gaul* would be too costly and challenging. Twenty years after the *Gaul* was lost, Stuart Randall, MP for Kingston upon Hull West, wrote to the Ministry of Defence to enquire about the feasibility of searching for the *Gaul*. In response, he received a letter from the MOD which claimed that this would be a "massive undertaking" as hundreds of square miles of seabed would have to be searched. This, combined with the harsh conditions of the Barents Seats and the fact that hundreds of wrecks littered the seabed meant that such a search would be prohibitively expensive and would not have a realistic chance of success, the MOD claimed.

Secrets of the Gaul

In 1997, the Norwegian public service broadcaster NKR joined with British television station Channel 4 to fund an expedition to find the *Gaul*. They commissioned a marine recovery team which used sonar to search the area where the *Rairo* had snagged its nets and, within hours, had located what they believed to be the wreck of the *Gaul*. A remotely operated vehicle (ROV) was then lowered 280 metres (918 ft) to the seabed which confirmed they had found the *Gaul*.

The discovery was broadcast in a documentary entitled *Secrets of the Gaul* was aired on Channel 4 in the UK in October 1997 as part of the broadcaster's long-running *Dispatches* series. Directed by Norman Fenton and featuring the journalist and writer Callum Macrae, the programme revealed that the *Gaul* was relatively intact, with its windows unbroken and its bridge mostly undamaged and trawl nets covered much of the vessel. The position of the rudder showed that the *Gaul* had been making a turn hard to port when it sank. The condition of the wreck disproved many of the conspiracy theories surrounding the loss of the vessel, such as the *Gaul* being destroyed by missiles or torpedoes, and offered hope to the crew's families that they would finally be able to learn the truth of what happened to the *Gaul*.

Secrets of the Gaul also revealed that the spy ship theories, which had been around since the unsatisfactory initial investigation in 1974, were based on truth. MP Bill Rodgers had categorically stated in the years following the loss of the *Gaul* (when he was Minister of State for Defence) that civilian crews were never tasked with spying on Soviet ship movements. This was not the case – trawler crews were given equipment and training to record and track the movements of Soviet vessels. It was revealed that Peter Nellist, the skipper of the *Gaul*, and Maurice Spurgeon, the mate, had both been trained to carry out surveillance for the Royal Navy in the late 1960s and early 1970s on vessels they had worked on before the *Gaul*. In 2000, Commander Timothy Clark, a member of the defence intelligence staff, was quoted in the *Guardian* as saying that it could not be known if members of the *Gaul*'s crew were involved in spying as "no records of trawler personnel involved in this activity exist in MoD files". Furthermore, Commander Clark revealed that training trawler crews to spy on Soviet warships was so common that a retired Royal Navy officer known only as Commander Brooks, who was also an MI6 intelligence officer, worked as a liaison between the Ministry of Defence and trawler crews between 1960 and 1971. There were also claims that this was formalised in a covert programme known as Operation Hornbeam, which gave trawler crews training enabling them to identify Soviet ships and those from other Warsaw Pact countries.

Even more shocking news came to light when news emerged that in 1972, the Royal Navy had placed personnel and satellite navigation equipment on the trawler FV *Invincible* and used the trawl nets of the vessel to try and recover a Soviet test missile that had been lost in the Barents Sea. Maurice Spurgeon had been the mate on the *Invincible* during this operation, which was not successful, although it may have been that the crew were not told the truth of the operation and believed that they were searching for a camera lost from an American submarine. Another attempt was made to recover the missile with the trawler FV *Lord Nelson* the following year, although this also failed.

This news seemed to vindicate the claims of many of the crew's family members who believed that the *Gaul* was playing a role in espionage, which would have made it a target of Soviet aggression. However, the footage obtained by the ROVs and broadcast on *The Secrets of the Gaul* did not back this up. The *Gaul* had clearly not been destroyed by a torpedo, missile, mine or naval gunfire, and there was no damage to the wreck to indicate it had been involved in a collision with a ship or submarine. The investigation team also ruled out the *Gaul* being sunk by heavy waves flooding the vessel, as the crew would have had enough time to issue a distress call if this was the case.

The reason for the loss of the *Gaul*, therefore, remained unknown. But with the new evidence that had been brought to light and the location of the wreck now known, John Prescott, Britain's Deputy Prime Minister at the time, took action. After two and a half decades, the UK government would finally authorize an investigation to discover exactly what happened to the *Gaul*.

New Investigations

The Marine Accident Investigation Branch – the UK government organisation which investigates marine accidents wherever they happen in the world – was comissioned to investigate the wreck of the Gaul in the summer of 1998. A team of MAIB investigators and experts from Southampton Oceanography Centre travelled to the site of the wreck, accompanied by several members of the crew's families who were permitted to attend to observe the investigation. A survey ship was used as the base of the operations, and multiple ROVs were used to examine the wreck. Some ROVs were fitted with video cameras to gain footage of the *Gaul*, while others had hydraulic hammers which allowed them to punch through windows and portholes to take images inside the ship, and another was fitted with shears to cut through the trawl nets which covered the *Gaul*.

In the forty-five hours of footage which was recorded by the ROVs, it could be seen that there was some damage to the bow, bulkheads and funnels of the *Gaul*, but this had been caused by water pressure, impact from striking the seabed, or trawlers dragging their nets over the wreck, and was not the cause of the sinking. There were also seabed cables near the wreck, but these were ruled out as playing any part in the loss of the *Gaul*. It was also established that some of the *Gaul*'s weathertight doors and hatches were in the open position. The ROVs were not able to locate any human remains, although the crew's family members were satisfied that every possible effort had been made to do so. The *Gaul*'s bell was also recovered during this investigation.

The data the investigation had gathered was used to carry out scale model tests and experiments to try and finally work out what caused the *Gaul* to sink. In late 1998 and early 1999, a one-forty-sixth scale model of the *Gaul* was constructed and tested in a hydrodynamics testing tank in a facility at Southampton Oceanography Centre. It was established during the tests that the *Gaul* was an "extremely seaworthy vessel", and one of the main theories that large waves breaking onto her trawl deck would have flooded the *Gaul* and caused her to sink was disproved by the model tests. However, it was calculated that very large waves of 22 metres (72 ft) could have capsized the *Gaul* if another factor which destabilized the vessel came into play. This could be unsecured cargo moving around inside the hold or additional water pouring in through open hatches and doors.

While valuable information had been gathered, the exact reason for the loss of the *Gaul* still eluded investigators. In 2002, the investigation was re-opened, and another even more extensive exploration of the wreck was planned with the underwater engineering and exploration company Subsea 7 commissioned to carry out the investigation. Subsea 7's multipurpose vessel MPSV *Seisranger* arrived at the site of the *Gaul* in July 2002 and remained there for twenty-four days. Nine different ROVs were used to survey the wreck, some of which were fitted with hydro-cutting technology and chainsaws which allowed them to cut through steel plates and wooden doors and gain access to the internal corridors and cabins of the *Gaul*. Altogether, 3,000 hours of footage of the wreck was recorded. During this investigation, the ROVs were also able to locate and collect samples of human remains from four men. When these were subjected to DNA tests, it was confirmed that they did come from members of the *Gaul*'s crew, finally putting to rest the belief that the men could have been captured by the Russians and held captive in the Soviet Union.

This new survey confirmed the findings of the 1998 investigation that the damage to the funnels and bow of the *Gaul* was not the reason for the vessel's sinking. It was also found that the trawl deck door was secured open, and the engine room escape door was also open, although it may have been moved into this position by a crewmember attempting to escape the vessel. The duff and offal chutes, located on the factory deck (below the trawl deck), were also in the open position. As the *Gaul* was a factory freezer trawler, the fish it caught were gutted and filleted before being frozen. The crew would dispose of the unusable and inedible guts and offal by placing them into chutes that emptied into the sea. Duffs are large sponge-like marine creatures which can be over 1 metre (3 ft) in diameter. Trawler crews considered them an annoyance as they caused congestion in the trawl nets and had to be sorted from the fish catch and then chopped into pieces before being disposed of down the chutes. Investigators believed that these chutes, which had not previously been considered important, played a major role in the loss of the *Gaul*.

The Loss of the *Gaul* Revealed

In 2004 the official re-opened formal investigation into the sinking of the *Gaul* was published. It stated that seizure by the Soviet military, hitting a mine, ice accumulation, deliberate sinking, a missile attack or torpedo attack, collision with another vessel, snagging a seabed obstruction and a submarine becoming entangled with the *Gaul*'s nets could all definitively be eliminated as causes of the sinking. While it was acknowledged that trawler crews did spy on Soviet ships, the investigation stated that there was no evidence that the *Gaul* was involved in spying in any way during its final voyage. The search for John Doone, who was supposedly seen in a bar in South Africa, was deemed a simple case of mistaken identity. The claims of microbiologist Mr Hendey that the *Gaul*'s lifebuoy lacked deep water plankton and had only ever been in shallow water were also discounted. The report explained that Mr Hendey had only received the lifebuoy three weeks after it was recovered, and there was no audit trail to explain where it had been during that time. It may have been the case that the lifebuoy was cleaned and washed before being given to Mr Hendey, explaining the freshwater algae.

The claim that the *Gaul* could have been capsized by very large waves was also discounted, as multiple waves would have needed to hit the *Gaul* in rapid succession, and this would have caused significant damage to the superstructure of the vessel, which was not present on the wreck. However, large waves striking the vessel, when combined with another factor, could explain why the *Gaul* capsized and sank. This additional factor was the *Gaul*'s duff and offal chutes. During the storm, they were left in the open position, with the skipper and crew seemingly unaware that this allowed large amounts of water into the vessel and flooded the factory deck. It was estimated that more than one hundred tons of water may have flowed into the *Gaul* through the duff and offal chutes, severely compromising the *Gaul*'s stability and taking the vessel "from a safe to critical scenario in twenty minutes".

This additional water had flooded into the *Gaul* when the sharp turn to port under full engine power was conducted. Under normal circumstances, even in a storm, the *Gaul* would have easily coped with this action, but performing this manoeuvre under these circumstances would have caused the additional water on board to surge to the starboard side of the ship, causing the *Gaul* to roll dangerously. This list, which the *Gaul* would ordinarily have been able to recover from, would have submerged the duff and offal chutes below the waterline, causing more water to flow into the factory deck. With more and more water flowing into the *Gaul* through the chutes, the vessel would have been unable to recover from the roll and would have capsized and then sunk, stern first, within a very short amount of time. The crew would have had no time to issue a distress call or launch the life rafts or lifeboat, and any crew members who were able to escape the sinking vessel by jumping into the sea would have succumbed to the cold and storm conditions within minutes of entering the water,.

Future Recommendations and Memorial to the *Gaul*

The MAIB investigation stated that the reason why the duff and offal chutes had not been secured shut was unclear – the flaps and watertight covers were functioning and could have been closed to prevent seawater ingress. The skipper, who had previously worked on trawlers which did not feature duff and offal chutes, may have simply been unaware of the importance of closing the chutes in storm conditions. The report made clear the importance of securing all hatches and chutes shut in bad weather and highlighted that the danger of allowing water to accumulate on the factory deck had not been made clear to the crew. The report made the following main recommendations:

- Warning signs should displayed stating that any chutes or other openings in the ship's sides should be closed unless they were in active use.
- It should be reiterated that the accumulation of water on the factory deck could destabilize the vessel.

- Pumps which could activate automatically should be fitted to remove water from the factory deck of trawlers of the type of the *Gaul*.
- CCTV should be fitted so the skipper/crew could monitor the factory deck when no one was present there.
- Warning lights should be used to indicate when chutes and openings on the sides of the ship were in the open position.

It was also acknowledged that the *Gaul* was lost decades before the report was published. Declining fish stocks and changes in commercial fishing methods meant that vessels of the type of the *Gaul* were unlikely to be built again, meaning that the recommendations were of limited relevance to the majority of fishing vessels operating in the early twenty-first century.

While many of the mysteries and conspiracy theories surrounding the *Gaul* have been resolved, questions remain. There can be no doubt that the British government concealed information about trawler crews being used to report and track the movements of Soviet ships. This, combined with the inexplicable reluctance of the government to search for the wreck of the *Gaul*, allowed conspiracy theories to take hold, which added immeasurable pain to the crew's families, who had no answers as to what caused the disaster. With decades now having passed since the *Gaul* was lost, it appears that such questions about the British government's conduct will never be answered.

In 2024, a series of events took place in Hull and North Shields to mark the fiftieth anniversary of the loss of the *Gaul*. This included the unveiling of a new mural, depicting the *Gaul* at sea, on the side of Hull Fishing Heritage Centre and a service in which the ship's bell, which had been recovered from the wreck, was sounded.

Chapter 2

The Eyemouth Fishing Disaster

In October 1881, several hundred men from the village of Eyemouth in the Scottish Borders travelled out into the North Sea to fish for haddock in oar and sail-powered fishing boats. Shortly after they reached their fishing grounds, a fierce storm set in. Few of the boats would make it back to Eyemouth, and in a single day, the town lost one-tenth of its male population.

Eyemouth is a town in Berwickshire on the south-east coast of Scotland. In the late 1800s, fishing was a significant part of the town's economy, with a large proportion of men from Eyemouth and the surrounding towns employed as fishermen and many others finding work connected to fishing, such as bait collecting, transporting catches and boat maintenance and repair.

While many fishermen caught mid-water species such as herring, the Eyemouth fishermen targeted species found on the seabed, with haddock making up the majority of their catches. They would travel to their fishing grounds many miles offshore in small, sail-powered boats, but in calm, windless conditions, they would have to row to reach their destination. None of the Eyemouth boats used trawl nets to catch their fish. Instead, hundreds of hooks were baited with mussels and then dropped down from the boats to the seabed. When the shoals of haddock were present, huge numbers of fish could be caught using this method, and the fishermen could make good incomes for themselves. However, as Peter Aitchison writes in the book *Black Friday*, life for these fishermen was precarious as their income would drop significantly if catches were poor. At other times, they would make no money at all if bad weather prevented them from going to sea. Aitchison writes "When the shoals were regular ... there was plenty to eat, and enough money to ensure that the bars, shebeens and grocery stores supplied liberal quantities to drink." But bad weather which prevented the men from going to sea, or the absence of the fish shoals would impact the men so badly that they and their families would be forced to seek support from charities and food from soup kitchens.

A further issue contributing to the disaster was the state of Eyemouth Harbour. The Church of Scotland required Eyemouth fishermen to pay tithes. This was effectively a tax of one-tenth of their income, and Eyemouth was the only place in Scotland where this was levelled at fishermen. The Eyemouth fishermen had, unsurprisingly, been outraged by this and were involved in a long-running dispute with the church to try and get the tithe payments stopped. While this dispute was ongoing, the fees for the maintenance of the harbour went unpaid. This led to the harbour falling into a state of disrepair, and the long-promised plans to deepen the harbour to improve the safety of vessels had yet to be started at the time of the disaster.

Storm Warnings

Due to poor weather conditions, the Eyemouth fishing fleet had been confined to port for a week before the disaster. With the men having made no income during this time, they were understandably keen to get to sea and begin catching fish on the morning of 14 October 1881. Conditions were calm and still, and the supplies of bait – mostly mussel, of which the fleet could use tens of thousands per day – would start going stale, costing the fishermen even more money if they did not fish that day. Furthermore, the lack of fishing over the previous week meant that the prices they would receive for the fish they did catch would be high, providing an additional incentive to get out to sea and fish. In *Black Friday*, Peter Aitchison writes that the older fishermen warned against going to sea that morning. The weather may have been calm but there had been storms the previous night, and barometers showed low air pressure – a sure sign that another storm was on its way.

But the younger men won the argument and forty-one boats of the haddock fishing fleet went to sea that morning. The fleet operated as a group, and once the decision was made to fish, everyone followed it, including the older men who advised against going to sea. While the fishing boats were equipped with sails, the weather for most of their journey was so still that there was not enough wind to power the vessels, meaning that the men had to row the twelve miles to their fishing grounds. After they set off, a telegram arrived at the post office in Eyemouth, warning of the incoming storm and stating that all fishing boats should remain in the harbour. But the telegram arrived too late for the Eyemouth fishermen.

The Storm Breaks

The men had reached their fishing grounds and just lowered the first of their fishing lines when the storm broke. Realising they would soon be in trouble, the men abandoned fishing and began to head back to shore. But the storm, which had begun as a gale, quickly transformed into what today would be classed as a European windstorm, and the boats, still many miles out to sea, were caught in the middle of it. Hurricane-force winds ripped the sails and masts from some vessels, while enormous waves slammed into the sides of the boats, with several capsizing. Desperately trying to control their boats as best they could, the majority of the surviving boats desperately headed toward the safety of the harbour, but a few took the opposite approach and headed away from the land further out to sea in an attempt to find calmer waters and wait out the storm.

Waves overturned some of the vessels as they tried to make their way back to Eyemouth, whereas others lost crewmembers who fell from their boats in the tumbling sea. Despite the storm making land and causing immense damage to the town of Eyemouth, ripping the roofs from houses and toppling over trees, the wives and children of the fishermen gathered at the harbour, frantically waiting to see if the boats would make it back.

The Hurkars are a series of low-lying rocks close to the entrance of Eyemouth Harbour. Exposed at low tide, they are a hazard to shipping, even in good weather. As the Eyemouth fleet began to return, they had to try to navigate past the Hurkars with little control over their boats in the winds and rising and falling seas. *Harmony* was the first boat to be wrecked against the Hurkars. It was smashed against the rocks by a huge wave, while the wives and children, lined up in the harbour barely 200 metres (650 ft) away, watched in horror. Further boats *Radiant* and *Press Home* were also lost as they tried to make their way into the harbour but were instead lifted by the heavy seas onto the Hurkars.

The effect on the watching families was devastating. Some had seen their fathers, sons and husbands lost at sea within sight of land, while others were left hoping against hope that the boats they were waiting for had somehow found some other way of surviving the storm. For a small number of the waiting women, this did turn out to be the case, with the boats *Enterprise, Success, White Star* and *Iona* all managing to make land safely further along the coast, with some of the fishermen able to send a telegram to Eyemouth to inform their families that they were safe.

Many of the women stayed out until late in the night, with some still there the following day, looking out to sea in the forlorn hope that their husbands would appear. Forty-five hours after the storm broke, one boat did return. The *Ariel Gazelle* was one of the few vessels which headed out further into the North Sea where the effects of the storm were less severe and waited for the storm's power to fade before heading to the harbour. But this was the only exception. Despite people keeping watch from Eyemouth Harbour for a week, and Royal Navy vessels eventually arriving to join the search, no further boats returned to Eyemouth.

Aftermath of the Disaster

In the days after the disaster, it emerged that 189 men had lost their lives – 129 were from Eyemouth, and the rest were from the surrounding towns of Burnmouth, Newhaven, Fisherrow, Cove, and St Abbs. Pieces of wrecked boats and body parts of fishermen continued to wash up on the beaches surrounding Eyemouth for months after the disaster, with the last not being recovered until March of the following year, five months after the incident. Peter Aitchison writes that the remaining fishermen from Eyemouth and the nearby fishing villages were left with the "necessary but ghoulish task" of dragging nets through the water to recover the bodies of their dead colleagues. The bodies were often in terrible condition, with only thirty-one bodies being suitable for a full burial. Aitchison writes that for the most part "Bits of men. Limbs, lumps of flesh, perhaps even pulped heads, were dragged up or washed to shore." They were taken away and buried, but Aitchison writes that the women of the town were not told about this.

Eyemouth had lost one-tenth of its men and would take over a century to return to its pre-disaster population level. In such a close-knit community, the effects were devastating, with many wives losing not just their husbands and children but many members of their extended families as well. Reports from the time estimated that 300 children lost their fathers in the disaster, and ninety-one women were widowed. However, the actual figures are now believed to be 178 children left fatherless and seventy-eight women left widowed.

The disaster was major news across the country, with all of the national newspapers reporting on the scale of the loss of life and the impact it would have on the town of Eyemouth. People across Britain began raising money for the survivors and the bereaved families, with donations coming from as far away as London. Queen Victoria reportedly sent a £100 donation, and Edward Marjoribanks, the MP for Berwickshire, sent £200. By Christmas following the disaster, around £50,000 had been raised for the people of Eyemouth, the equivalent of more than £5 million in 2024.

But the surviving fishermen of Eyemouth could not wait for charity to come in. On 31 October, just two weeks after the disaster, the fishermen, in boats including the *Ariel Gazelle*, went back to sea to fish for haddock, although they would no longer go to sea on a Friday out of respect for those who had lost their lives. The 14 October 1881 became known as Black Friday in Eyemouth and the surrounding towns.

Memorials

An 1884 publication entitled *Wrecks and Reminiscences of St Andrews Bay* by George Bruce of St Andrews states that a memorial service was held in 1882 on the anniversary of the disaster. It reads:

> A memorial service was preached in the Parish Church, and in the Free Church at night, being the anniversary of the disaster. During the service, the shops were closed and business was suspended, the funeral bell tolled, the organ played *The Dead March in Saul*.

A memorial to the disaster depicting a broken sail mast was erected in Eyemouth, and in 2016, on the 135th anniversary of the disaster, a new sculpture commemorating the tragedy was unveiled. Entitled *Women and Bairns*, the £250,000 sculpture overlooks the bay and consists of a 5-metre-long (16 ft) wall with small bronze figures representing the women and children of Eyemouth looking out to sea. The 4.5-metre-long (15 ft) Eyemouth Tapestry, which memorialises every crewmember and boat involved in the disaster, is also on display in Eyemouth Museum.

Chapter 3

Ehime Maru and USS *Greeneville* Collision

In February 2001, the *Ehime Maru*, a Japanese trawler and fishing training ship, was making its way to fishing grounds in the Pacific Ocean. At the same time, in the waters beneath the *Ehime Maru*, the submarine USS *Greeneville* was carrying out manoeuvres as part of a programme for distinguished guests on board. A series of mistakes and oversights from the crew and command team of the American submarine would lead to the loss of the Japanese vessel and the deaths of nine of its crew.

The USS *Greeneville* was commissioned into the US Navy in 1996, the second-last of the sixty-two nuclear-powered Los Angeles-class submarines built between 1972 and 1995. The USS *Greeneville* had a submerged displacement of 7,177 tons and was armed with Mark 48 torpedoes and Tomahawk cruise missiles. In early 2001, the USS *Greeneville* was based at Pearl Harbor in Hawaii and was commanded by Scott Waddle, a 38-year-old Texan who was seen as a rising star in the US Navy, having beaten 140 other officers to be selected as the Commanding Officer of the *Greeneville*. At the time of the incident, the *Greeneville* was participating in the US Navy's Distinguished Visitor Embarkation programme. This was a scheme where politicians, journalists and business people deemed important or significant were invited to observe life on board US submarines, surface vessels and military bases. The programme aimed to raise awareness of the day-to-day life of military personnel and gain support for the US armed forces.

Prelude to the Disaster

Just before 8.00 am on the morning of 9 February 2001, the USS *Greeneville* departed Pearl Harbor, travelling on the surface with the sixteen civilian visitors on board in addition to its crew of twelve officers and ninety-eight enlisted men. The schedule for the day would see the visitors shown around the submarine, have lunch with the commanding officer and then experience a deep dive and further high-speed manoeuvres before returning to Pearl Harbor at 3.00 pm. It was acknowledged by the senior officers on board the *Greeneville* that the schedule for the day was "fairly tight" with "little time to mess around." This was exacerbated by the lunch having to take place across two sittings of eight visitors each, as the Commanding Officer's wardroom was too small to accommodate all of the visitors at once.

The *Ehime Maru* was a 58-metre (190 ft) long Uwajima Fisheries High School training vessel which had a gross tonnage of 741 tons. Owned and operated by the government of Japan's Ehime Prefecture, the *Ehime Maru* allowed students who wanted a career in commercial fishing to gain seagoing experience. It was crewed by a total of thirty-five – a mix of students, instructors and experienced fishermen. The *Ehime Maru* was captained by Hisao Ōnishi, a seafarer with forty years of experience on merchant ships and fishing vessels. He had commanded the *Ehime Maru* since its first voyage five years previously.

At midday on 9 February, the *Ehime Maru* left Pearl Harbor and began its journey to its fishing grounds several hundred miles out into the Pacific Ocean. This was the second part of a 74-day training exercise that had started in Japan on 10 January. The weather was generally good, although isolated thunderstorms and rough seas were predicted a few days into their journey. The *Ehime Maru* continued on its way at a steady speed of around 11 knots (12.5 mph).

Distinguished Visitor Embarkation Programme and High-speed Manoeuvres

On board the *Greeneville*, the visitors experienced the normal operation of the submarine. At approximately 11.00 am, the *Greeneville* submerged to a depth of 213 metres (700 ft), and water samples were collected and given to the visitors in small containers as souvenirs of their time on board. Some civilians were then allowed to sit at the submarine's controls accompanied by a crewmember while simple direction and depth changes were carried out. A short time after this the first lunch sitting began, but it soon became clear that they were overrunning their schedule, possibly because some of the visitors came from the same state as Commander Waddle and they had engaged in conversation for longer than expected. This led to a discussion between the submarine's senior officers over the plan for the rest of the day, with the executive officer (the second in command) stating that they would have to forego the high-speed manoeuvres and return to Pearl Harbor immediately to make the 3.00 pm deadline. When Waddle, who had been signing photographs to give to the visitors as gifts, was informed of this, he overruled the decision and stated that the high-speed manoeuvres would be carried out. When he was told they would not return on time, he said: "Well, I guess we are going to be late."

At this point, the sonar of the *Greeneville* picked up several vessels on the surface, one of which was the *Ehime Maru*. However, this was designated as a distant contact, meaning it was at least 18,290 metres (20,000 yds) away and was not considered a hazard to the *Greeneville*. Indeed, the *Greeneville*'s crewmembers responsible for tracking surface vessels believed their workloads to be light, as they never had to follow more than a few surface contacts – in times of high workload, tracking between twenty and thirty surface vessels would be necessary. But one problem was that the *Greeneville*'s Analog-Video Signal Display Unit (AVSDU) was not functioning. The AVSDU replicates what appears on the sonar room monitors in the control room allowing the commanding officer to see what is happening on the sonar without leaving his post. While this would later prove to be a major contributing factor to the incident, the lack of a working AVSDU was not considered a significant problem at the time.

By 1.15 pm, the *Greeneville* was ready to begin the high-speed manoeuvres. The Commanding Officer had not discussed surface contacts with any other officers or the sonar crew but did spend time telling the visitors the best places to stand to observe what would happen. In the official investigation into the incident, *Greeneville* crew members would later say that civilians blocked their view of vital equipment used to monitor the submarine's position in relation to the surface contacts and that Waddle "seemed frustrated that he couldn't start the manoeuvre right away."

The first manoeuvre consisted of steep, angled depth changes at high speed, during which Waddle gave a running commentary of what was happening to the visitors. During this time, the crew stated that two of the surface contacts could not be constantly tracked, and the inability to see the equipment the civilians were blocking meant they could not accurately keep track of the *Greeneville*'s position. Another crewmember later told investigators that the sonar technicians had to discuss the surface contacts with their colleagues and answer questions from the guests at the same time. After the depth changes, the next manoeuvre consisted of a series of high-speed turns. The crew later stated that this made the lines on the sonar display "look like spaghetti" as the submarine moved away from and then closer to the surface contacts, making the contacts significantly more challenging to track.

Surface Contacts

Just after 1.30 pm the *Greeneville* stopped the high-speed manoeuvres, decreased speed and ascended to just below the surface. The purpose of this was to maintain a steady speed for a minimum of three minutes to allow the crew to gain an accurate picture of the surface contacts and the *Greeneville*'s position relative to them. However, data would later show that the *Greeneville* only remained on this course for ninety-one seconds, only twenty seconds of which were spent travelling at a steady speed and depth. Regulations stated that a briefing between Waddle (as the Commanding Officer), the senior officers, and other key personnel must be held to ensure there was consensus on the location of surface contacts. Waddle ignored this, and the briefing did not take place. A senior officer on board during the incident told the later investigation that he "would never think of not doing a periscope-depth brief[ing]" but trusted Waddle to take them to periscope depth without a briefing due to Waddle's experience. Waddle then gave the order for the *Greeneville* to proceed to a depth of 18 metres (60 ft). This was periscope depth and would allow Waddle and other senior officers to visually check the area the *Greeneville* was in for surface vessels. The submarine's periscope broke the surface and completed eight revolutions, with the senior officer who conducted the search reporting that no surface contacts were nearby. It later transpired that conditions were hazy, and the white hull of the *Ehime Maru* would have made the vessel difficult to see, especially in the short time the *Greeneville* spent at periscope depth.

During this time, the *Greeneville*'s crew noted that the signal-to-noise ratio was increasing – a clear sign that surface contacts were closing in on them. The situation then became more complicated when a new surface contact appeared on the sonar. During this time, Waddle was not able to see the sonar screen from the command room due to the malfunctioning AVSDU. As this was happening, the sonar crew were gaining a better picture of the surface contacts, although one of them would later admit that this was "rushed." It was concluded that the *Ehime Maru* was significantly closer than they had previously believed, and its range was changed from 14,630 metres (16,000 yds) away to 3,660 metres (4,000 yds). Waddle then carried out his own periscope search and agreed that the previous search was accurate and there were no major surface contacts close to their location (he would later admit that he had been concentrating his search in the area where their most recent contact had been picked up, explaining how he missed the presence of the *Ehime Maru*). Based on Waddle carrying out a periscope search and seeing no surface contacts, the sonar crew once again changed the location of the *Ehime Maru*, this time placing it 8,230 metres (9,000 yds) from them. In reality, it was just 2,040 metres (2,240 yds) away.

Emergency Ballast Tank Blow and Collision

The *Greeneville* then dived deep as the crew prepared to bring the vessel back to the surface by performing an emergency ballast tank blow. This is a manoeuvre where water is rapidly forced out of the main ballast tanks by high-pressure air, causing the submarine to quickly rise at a sharp angle to the surface. As the submarine was being readied, Waddle allowed one of the civilian visitors to sit in the helmsman's chair while another visitor, under supervision from a crewmember, was permitted to operate the valves which released the high-pressure air to force the water from the ballast tanks. Waddle then started another running commentary of the events for the benefit of the visitors. As this was being carried out the *Ehime Maru* was moving ever closer to the *Greeneville*'s position. When the civilian visitor operated the lever to perform the emergency ballast tank blow, and the *Greeneville* rapidly rose to the surface, the submarine was directly underneath the *Ehime Maru*.

As the *Greeneville* reached the surface, there was a loud banging noise, which caused the entire submarine to shudder and Waddle to shout, "What the hell was that?" On the surface, the stern of the *Ehime Maru* had been lifted out of the water as the *Greeneville*'s rudder – which was specially reinforced to enable the submarine to break through Arctic ice – had struck and then sliced through the hull of the *Ehime Maru*. The *Ehime Maru* briefly settled on the surface and then lost all power as the water around it turned black with diesel and oil which flowed from the vessel.

It immediately became evident to Hisao Ōnishi, the captain of the *Ehime Maru,* that his ship had suffered catastrophic damage and was rapidly sinking. Three crewmembers on the lower decks and engine room (which were beneath the waterline) tried to scramble to safety, but only one was able to reach a set of ladders and climb to a hatch which led to the upper decks. The other two were forced back by the waves of diesel and seawater which surged along the deck. They were still trapped on the lower levels of the ship as it sank to the seabed. Nine students in the cabins and crew's mess at the time of the collision waded through a waist-deep mixture of diesel and seawater to reach the open upper deck where they could grab lifejackets and abandon ship. Other crewmembers tried to climb up the *Ehime Maru's* superstructure as the vessel sank beneath the water, but many were knocked into the sea by waves that reached heights of 4 metres (12 ft). Others were dragged underwater by the sinking vessel but floated to the surface when their automatically inflating lifejackets deployed. When the *Ehime Maru* was 25 metres (80 ft) below the surface, the vessel's lifeboat successfully detached and floated to the surface, and the survivors, almost all of whom were covered in oil and diesel, could swim to the lifeboat and climb in. Just five minutes passed between the collision and the *Ehime Maru* sinking entirely beneath the waves.

Rescue Attempts

The *Greeneville* immediately radioed the Pearl Harbor naval base and requested emergency assistance. The crew of the *Greeneville* then attempted their own rescue, with the wardroom being made into a makeshift medical room, and divers were prepared to enter the water as the crew searched for survivors using both of the submarine's periscopes. However, the sea conditions were working against the *Greeneville*. The hatches on the main deck of the *Greeneville* could not be opened as the large waves would swamp the submarine. This was exacerbated by the fact that the *Greeneville* was still low in the water as completely emptying the ballast tanks was a process which took around thirty minutes. This meant that the only access to the submarine was by using a rope ladder with plastic steps to climb into the submarine through the sail.

The *Greeneville* approached one of the lifeboats, and an officer attempted to direct some of the survivors onto the submarine, but the language barrier, along with the rough sea conditions, prevented this from happening. Waddle then became worried that the movement of the *Greeneville* was creating further waves which could potentially capsize the *Ehime Maru*'s lifeboat. This, along with the difficulty in bringing survivors on board the submarine, and the belief that the Coast Guard and other rescue vessels would soon be arriving, led Waddle to give the order for the *Greeneville* to leave the scene of the collision and return to Pearl Harbor.

The first Coast Guard helicopter reached the survivors around forty-five minutes after the collision and surveyed the scene. A short time later, two small Coast Guard vessels arrived, and the helicopter was able to airlift some of the survivors with more severe injuries onto the Coast Guard vessels. A helicopter crewmember was also lowered to administer first aid to survivors who remained on the *Ehime Maru*'s lifeboat. Within an hour, a larger vessel, the Island-class Coast Guard cutter *Assateague,* was also on its way to the scene, as was a C-130 aircraft which would take overall command of the rescue effort. Eventually, all of the survivors were rescued by the Coast Guard and taken to Hawaii for medical treatment. The main injuries suffered by the survivors were broken bones, hypothermia and eye and throat irritations caused by swimming in water covered with diesel and oil. Once the situation had stabilized, Hisao Ōnishi counted the survivors and calculated that nine people were missing. While the search for further survivors continued for many days, and the search for bodies for weeks, no trace of the nine missing crewmembers was found.

One week after the incident, on 16 February, the wreck of the *Ehime Maru* was located, sitting upright on the seabed, around 915 metres (1,000 yds) from the scene of the collision. Remotely operated underwater vehicles (ROVs) were used to search the wreck, but no bodies were found. On 2 March the search for survivors was officially called off.

Aftermath, Inquiry and Admiral's Mast

Immediately after the collision, Waddle was stood down from his position as commander of the *Greeneville*, and a court of inquiry began in March 2001 in Hawaii. While this was akin to a civil court case, it could lead to a court-martial if the military personnel involved were found responsible for wrongdoing. Waddle attended and was represented by Charles Gittins, a former Marine Corps officer turned lawyer who specialized in defending military clients. Families of the crew of the *Ehime Maru* were also present. Waddle testified at the court of inquiry, as did *Ehime Maru* crewmembers who survived the collision.

The court of inquiry ruled that the captain and crew of the *Greeneville* were solely responsible for the incident and that no equipment failure on either the *Greeneville* or the *Ehime Maru* played a role in the collision. It concluded that the incident was not caused by "deliberate or willful misconduct" by the crew of the *Greeneville* but instead by a combination of errors and negligences from the crew. Waddle was identified as the main culprit, with the court stating that his failure to keep to schedule led to the crew feeling they had to rush through standard safety procedures which were in place to prevent such an incident from happening. Further criticisms were levelled at the submarine's surface contact team for their failure to work together and pass on information regarding the surface contact locations to Waddle and other senior officers. Waddle was personally criticized for becoming overinvolved in entertaining the guests on board to the extent that standard operating procedures were not followed. The inquiry concluded that had Waddle and the crew of the *Greeneville* followed standard procedures, it would have been likely that the collision would have been avoided.

Despite its damning verdict, the recommendations made by the inquiry were lenient. It did not recommend that Waddle was court-martialled, saying that his actions were characterized by negligence and carelessness rather than criminal intent. It also stated a factor in reaching this decision was his long service in the US Navy and the capability and competence

Waddle had shown in the years before the incident. Instead of a court-martial, the inquiry recommended that Waddle receive an Admiral's Mast. This is a form of non-judicial punishment issued by the US Navy to officers who have behaved improperly but have not shown criminal intent or deliberate misconduct. When the Admiral's Mast took place, the Pacific Fleet commander, Admiral Thomas B. Fargo, found Waddle guilty of dereliction of duty and negligence, which put his vessel in danger. He was given an official reprimand, a small fine, and told that it was expected that he would retire from the US Navy.

Other officers on the *Greeneville* were criticized for failing to keep an overview of the overall situation, failure to track surface contacts accurately and allowing civilian guests to get in the way of crewmembers and essential equipment. Several were demoted and others were made to requalify before resuming their supervisory positions.

Recovery of the Wreck and Later Events

In October 2001, a large-scale operation was initiated to recover the wreck of the *Ehime Maru*. The diving support and recovery vessel *Rockwater 2* was used to raise the *Ehime Maru* off the seabed, and it was then moved to a shallow water area off the coast of Hawaii. A joint team of US and Japanese divers searched the wreck and recovered eight of the missing bodies. The body of the ninth crewmember has never been found.

With the wreck now surveyed, the extent of the damage caused to the *Ehime Maru* also became apparent. It was established that a gouge, almost 1 metre (3 ft) wide, ran across the starboard side of the vessel. This breached the *Ehime Maru's* engine room and student lounge and also sliced through multiple fuel tanks. A 2005 report into the collision, which the United States National Transportation Safety Board compiled, found that damage caused to the *Ehime Maru* was so extensive that there was nothing the crew of the Japanese vessel could have done to prevent the ship from sinking. The event was also considered so unusual that there were no proposals to change the design of civilian vessels in light of the incident. A later damage report of the *Greeneville* would show that the submarine had a damaged and dented rudder and acoustic tiles (rubber or polymer tiles which absorb and reduce sonar signals) had been ripped from the submarine. Repairs to the *Greeneville* cost $1.44 million. As of 2024, the USS *Greeneville* is still in active service with the US Navy.

Japanese-US relations were badly affected in the aftermath of the *Ehime Maru*'s sinking, with many of the survivors, bereaved family members and Japanese officials questioning why the crew of the *Greeneville*, and Waddle in particular, had been given such light punishments for the role they played in the incident. In the months following the collision, questions continued to be asked by both Japanese and American media outlets as to why so many civilians were present on a US submarine as it conducted dangerous manoeuvres and why Waddle had not had to face a court-martial. This strained diplomatic relations between Japan and the USA, with tensions only easing the following year when the US government offered a financial aid package to compensate the families of the victims and pay for a new vessel to replace the *Ehime Maru*.

Despite the severity of the *Greeneville* and *Ehime Maru* collision, the US Navy made relatively minor changes to the Distinguished Visitor Embarkation programme. A review of the manoeuvres which submarines undertook with civilians on board was carried out, but this stopped short of banning any specific manoeuvres, such as the emergency ballast tank blow which caused the collision. Furthermore, there was no ban on civilians being present in the control room or any other areas of the submarine during its operations. Instead, vague guidance that the commanding officer needed to ensure that civilians did not interfere with the safe operation of the ship was issued, along with an instruction that one crewmember would work as a tour escort for every four to eight guests. While an instruction that civilians should not operate any of the submarine's equipment or controls was issued, this was caveated with the exception that it could be permitted if it was performed under the supervision of a qualified crewmember and a senior navy officer had given permission.

In late 2002, Waddle made a controversial visit to Japan. The US government opposed the visit, and Waddle was prohibited from making the journey until he had formally resigned from the US Navy. In Japan, he personally apologized to some of the victim's families, but several families refused to meet with him. The *Ehime Maru* Memorial Association (EMMA) was established in late 2001, and a memorial was built at Kaka'ako Waterfront Park in Hawaii the following year. A service attended by members of the victims' families and local dignitaries is held at the memorial on the anniversary of the incident every year.

After his enforced retirement from the US Navy, Scott Waddle reportedly spent ten months out of work before finding employment as a project manager with an energy company. In 2002, his book, *The Right Thing*, co-authored with Ken Abraham, was published. In the book, he told his life story and explained the *Ehime Maru* collision and aftermath from his perspective. Following the publication of the book, he reinvented himself as a public speaker. As of 2024, the website The Speakers Group states that Waddle is an "inspirational leader with uncompromising ethical standards" and that the audiences he speaks to will "learn pursuit of integrity against all odds" [sic]. The fee for booking him as a speaker is listed as $10,000 - £14,999 (£8,000 - £12,000).

Chapter 4

The *Bugaled Breizh*

The *Bugaled Breizh* was a French trawler which sank in mysterious circumstances in the English Channel in January 2004, with all five crewmembers losing their lives. There has been much speculation over what caused the loss of the vessel, with claims that a submarine engaged in NATO exercises collided with its nets and dragged the *Bugaled Breizh* beneath the waves. Subsequent investigations have stated this did not happen, but many of the crewmembers' families believe that the truth about the fate of *Bugaled Breizh* has yet to come to light.

The *Bugaled Breizh* was a trawler that operated out of Loctudy in Brittany in northwestern France. It was constructed in 1987, and at 24 metres (79 ft) in length and with a gross tonnage of 104 tons, it was a relatively large trawler which targeted species which lived on the seabed, such as cod, haddock and squid. The name *Bugaled Breizh* translates to 'Children of Brittany' in the Breton language.

The Days before the Disaster

On 7 January 2004, the *Bugaled Breizh* left the port of Le Guilvinec with another French fishing boat, the *Eridan*. The two vessels would often fish the same waters within close proximity of each other as Yves Gloaguen, captain of the *Bugaled Breizh*, and Serge Cossec, captain of the *Eridan*, knew each other well. They were scheduled to remain at sea for two weeks before returning to France. The *Bugaled Breizh* and the *Eridan* fished the waters of the English Channel without incident, with their catch being made up mostly of squid. Typically, the *Bugaled Breizh* would conduct six tows (the process of dragging the trawl nets along the seabed) every twenty-four hours, with the crew's breaks and rest periods based around this schedule. After a few days of fishing, the weather began to deteriorate to such an extent that both the *Bugaled Breizh* and the *Eridan* could not continue fishing, and both vessels made their way to Newlyn Harbour in Cornwall to shelter on 11 January. They remained there until the weather cleared, leaving on 13 January to sail back into the English Channel off the coast of southwest England, where they resumed fishing.

The *Bugaled Breizh* and the *Eridan* continued to fish within three or four miles of each other for the next few days. While the sea was rough, with swells of 2 - 3 metres (6 - 9 ft) and moderate wind speed, there was no threat to the vessels, and the conditions were perfectly safe for fishing. At 11.00 am (UK time) on 15 January, the captain of the *Bugaled Breizh* radioed the *Eridan* and said they were moving further to the south, believing that the fishing would be more productive there.

Emergency Messages

At 12.23 pm, Cossec was in the wheelhouse of the *Eridan* when he received an urgent call on the VHF radio from the *Bugaled Breizh*. Yves Gloaguen said that his boat was sinking and he required urgent assistance. Cossec asked for their location and then told Gloaguen that he should release their life raft, but Gloaguen only said that they were sinking several more times and gave no further information. Cossec rushed to the crew's quarters and gave the order to haul the trawl nets and ready the *Eridan* to sail to the *Bugaled Breizh*'s location at full speed. When he returned to the radio, Gloaguen repeated that he was sinking. Cossec said he heard a "crackling" sound and then lost radio contact altogether. Cossec issued a mayday call and set off on the forty-minute journey to the location of the *Bugaled Breizh*.

The *Eridan* arrived at the scene at around 13.15 pm. There was no sign of the *Bugaled Breizh*, but there was an oil slick and debris floating on the surface. Cossec used the *Eridan*'s fish-finding sonar to search the seabed and immediately located the wreck of the *Bugaled Breizh* 90 metres (295 ft) below the surface, with two thick columns of diesel fuel streaming upwards from the vessel. Cossec began to search for survivors and was soon joined by a British fishing boat, the *Silver Dawn*, which had heard the mayday call and broke off from fishing to assist. A distress beacon had been released from the *Bugaled Breizh*, which had sent a distress signal to Falmouth Maritime Rescue Coordination Centre (MRCC) in Cornwall. Staff there then radioed all vessels in the area, instructing them to make their way to the beacon's location. HMS *Tyne*, a Royal Navy River-class offshore patrol vessel and an RNLI rescue boat from the Lizard Lifeboat station in Cornwall also responded to the message and confirmed to Falmouth MRCC that they were heading to the scene. HNLMS *Dolfijn*, a Walrus-class submarine of the Royal Netherlands Navy was around 12 nautical miles (14 miles/22 km) away when it picked up the signal from the *Bugaled Breizh*'s distress beacon. The commander of the *Dolfijn* also radioed Falmouth MRCC to say that he was heading to the scene to assist in the search. The MRCC then contacted RNAS Culdrose to ask for a helicopter to be sent to the area to search from the air and by 1.00 pm a Sea King helicopter had been launched.

Rescue Operation

At the peak of the rescue effort, thirteen ships and two helicopters were searching 329 square kilometres (127 sq. miles) of the English Channel for survivors. The Royal Navy Sea King helicopter located a life raft on the surface and Leading Aircrewman Darren Hall was lowered to the raft to investigate and confirmed that the life raft was empty. The crew of the *Silver Dawn* found mooring rope floating on the surface, which they recovered, and the crew of the *Eridan* reported that they also found a life raft which was fully inflated with no one inside, two life rings, which they collected, and the *Bugaled Breizh*'s distress beacon. It was initially believed that the *Eridan* had found a second life raft from the *Bugaled Breizh*, but it would later emerge that this second life raft did not detach and the Sea King helicopter and the *Eridan* had both seen the same life raft. Eventually, the Sea King helicopter located a figure floating on the surface of the sea and Hall was again lowered down and recovered the *Bugaled Breizh* crewmember Pascal le Floch. While CPR was attempted as le Floch was flown to the Royal Cornwall Hospital, this was not successful and he was pronounced dead on arrival. After refuelling, the Sea King returned to the area, and later in the afternoon, the body of Yves Gloaguen was also recovered and taken to Cornwall.

The search continued, but darkness had set in, weather conditions were deteriorating with the windspeed picking up, and the size of the waves increasing to 3 – 4 metres (10 – 13 ft). While the search was officially suspended at 5.00 pm, some vessels, including the *Eridan*, continued searching until 7.00 pm, but no further survivors or bodies were found. The following morning, the search and rescue operation resumed with helicopters and a French Navy Breguet Atlantique reconnaissance aircraft surveying the area, but no survivors were located. By the afternoon of 16 January, it became clear that there were no further survivors from the *Bugaled Breizh* and the search and rescue operation was ended.

Investigations Begin

On 17 January, the French Navy minehunter *Andromède* left the port city of Brest in Brittany and headed to the wreck of the *Bugaled Breizh*, arriving the following day. A senior police officer who had been tasked with investigating the loss of the vessel was on board, along with Michel

Douce, the owner of the *Bugaled Breizh*, the President of the Brittany Sea Fisheries Committee, and investigators from BEAmer (Bureau d'Enquêtes sur les Événements de Mer) – the French equivalent of the UK's Marine Accident Investigation Branch (MAIB). They located the *Bugaled Breizh* on the seabed and a self-propelled mini-submarine, which was designed for anti-mine operations, was used to examine the wreck. As the *Bugaled Breizh* was lying on her port side, they could only observe the starboard side and the trawl nets, with images and video being transmitted back to the *Andromède*. Although there was some damage to the hull, no apparent cause of the vessel's sinking could be established through this preliminary investigation.

Initially, the *Bugaled Breizh* was believed to have succumbed to the weather conditions. This was soon rejected by the crew's families and other French fishermen who stated that the *Bugaled Breizh* was a large, robust trawler specifically designed to operate in rough seas and was manned by an experienced crew who knew how to cope with the conditions. Attention then turned to other ships which were operating in the area at the time, and a collision with another vessel was put forward as the most likely explanation for the loss of the *Bugaled Breizh*.

In a press conference on 19 January, just four days after the sinking, French prosecutor Roland Eisch claimed that the underwater images the *Andromède* had captured provided the answer as to what sank the *Bugaled Breizh*. He said that there was clear evidence of an "Extremely violent impact on the vessel's starboard bow, consistent with ramming by a large and powerful vessel of the container ship type, which caused the trawler to sink extremely rapidly." When this news reached Brittany, the BBC said that the reaction from the fishing community was one of fury. Michel Cap, director of the Loctudy Sea Rescue Service, said the actions of the cargo ship allegedly involved in the incident amounted to "murderous behaviour." Roland Eisch said that it was likely to be a foreign vessel that struck the *Bugaled Breizh*, and failing to stop to rescue the crew meant that a criminal offence had been committed. He went on to say an "international warrant will be issued … with a request for extradition once the guilty party is traced." Eisch also used the press conference to rule out some of the other theories which were beginning to emerge to explain the loss of the vessel. He said that as the trawl nets were visible, they could not have become snagged on an underwater obstruction, and despite a NATO exercise taking place nearby, the location of all warships in the area was accounted for, leaving a collision with a commercial vessel as the only possible explanation.

Despite the forcefulness of Eisch's claims, they were based on flimsy evidence. Although the underwater photographs showed some damage to the starboard side of the hull, they did not provide conclusive proof that there had been a collision with any ship, as they were likely caused by impact with the seabed. Furthermore, Yves Gloaguen did not mention a collision with another vessel when he radioed the *Eridan* to ask for help – something he almost certainly would have done if this had occurred. This did not stop investigations into the ship collision theory from continuing, with a cargo ship, the *Seattle Trader,* a Philippine-flagged bulk carrier, being identified as a suspect vessel due to its presence in the English Channel at the time the *Bugaled Breizh* sank. The French authorities went public with their desire to investigate the *Seattle Trader* in mid-February 2004. But by this time it was already on its way to China. A diplomatic incident occurred when the Egyptian government failed to detain the *Seattle Trader* as it passed through the Suez Canal, despite instructions from the French government to do so. French minister Dominique Bussereau said it was "incomprehensible" that the Egyptian authorities chose to ignore the French requests to stop the vessel, although it later emerged that this may have been down to a breakdown in communications between the two nations, rather than the Egyptian authorities rejecting the French government's request. French investigators were eventually able to inspect the *Seattle Trader* when it reached its destination in China. But after examining the vessel's hull and paintwork, it was announced that the investigators were satisfied that it played no role in the incident.

Refloating of the Wreck and the BEAmer Report

In June 2004 the company Stolt Offshore was tasked with raising the wreck of the *Bugaled Breizh* to the surface and transporting it to Brest. This was an extremely difficult task as the seabed the *Bugaled Breizh* was resting on had shifted since the vessel sank, and the wreck had been disturbed as the nets of other trawlers had snagged it. An attempt to refloat the *Bugaled Breizh* in late June was unsuccessful, with the wreck being raised 10 metres (33ft) up and then falling back to the seabed, causing damage to the stern and propellors. In mid-July 2004, Stolt Offshore successfully refloated the wreck, which was then transported to Brest Arsenal – a military base on the banks of the Penfeld River in Brittany. The body of a third crewmember, Patrick Gloaguen, was found on board during the salvage operation. The bodies of the other two crewmembers, Georges Lemetayer and Eric Guillamet have never been recovered.

With the *Bugaled Breizh* now in a dry dock, investigators from BEAmer could carry out a full analysis of the wreck. The damage from the failed refloating attempt and trawl nets made this more difficult, but investigators could still carry out a detailed study of the vessel. The damage to the hull, which led the French prosecutor to claim that there had been a collision with another ship, was confirmed to be caused by contact with the seabed and there were no traces of paint or metal-on-metal contact from another ship. Other damage to the *Bugaled Breizh*, such as a small diamond-shaped hole and vertical cracks in the hull's outer plating, were deemed too minor to have caused the sinking and were likely to have been caused by general wear and tear.

While the *Bugaled Breizh* was refloated in 2004, the BEAmer report was not published until 2007. In the intervening years, speculation that a submarine was responsible for the loss of the *Bugaled Breizh* began to grow. This was sparked by the news that the submarine HNLMS *Dolfijn* was active in the area where the *Bugaled Breizh* sank and intensified when it became known that a NATO exercise was being conducted nearby. With the French and British governments claiming that no military vessels were anywhere near the *Bugaled Breizh*, the Brittany fishermen's committee and the families of the *Bugaled Breizh*'s crew commissioned a team of French marine experts to carry out their own investigation into the disaster. The BBC reported that spokespeople for the families said that they believed a submarine could have snagged the nets or warp wires of the *Bugaled Breizh*. One of the investigators employed by the families stated in a press conference in 2005:

> The trawler rears up immediately and sinks from the back end very quickly ... The submarine can resume its course without too much damage and furthermore the accident goes unnoticed by most of the crew ... [We have the] conviction that the *Bugaled Breizh* was pulled down by a submarine.

Another independent investigation by French television channel FR3 also concluded that a submarine caused the *Bugaled Breizh* to sink and went as far as identifying HMS *Turbulent*, a Trafalgar-class nuclear-powered submarine of the Royal Navy, as being responsible. The British government immediately rejected this, with the Royal Navy stating that HMS *Turbulent* had been stationed at the Devonport Naval Base at the time of the incident, and the closest Royal Navy submarine was HMS *Torbay*, which was over 100 miles (160 km) away.

In 2007, the BEAmer report was finally released. It ruled out a collision with a surface vessel of any kind due to there being no damage or paint from another ship anywhere on the hull of the *Bugaled Breizh* and Yves Gloaguen making no mention of a collision when radioing the *Eridan* for help. The trawl nets being snagged on an undersea obstruction were also eliminated as a cause of the disaster, as the seabed in the area being trawled was clear. While there were undersea cables in the area, it was calculated that the *Bugaled Breizh* never came within 570 metres (620 yds) of them, and if the cables had been snagged they would have shown significant signs of damage. Most pertinently, the report stated that a submarine colliding with the trawl nets or warp wires did not cause the sinking. The nets were found close to the wreck, and if a submarine had collided with them, they would have been found in a completely different location. Furthermore, the trawl nets and warps would have shown damage if a submarine had collided with them, and such damage was completely absent.

With multiple theories for the sinking of the *Bugaled Breizh* being ruled out, the BEAmer report stated that a 'soft snag' was the reason for the loss of the vessel. A soft snag happens when the nets of a trawler become embedded in the sand or mud of the seabed. Usually, trawlers can simply pull out of a soft snag by increasing engine power, but the report found that the combination of weather and sea conditions caused the soft snag to result in the sinking of the *Bugaled Breizh*. This happened as *Bugaled Breizh* was engaged in fishing in rough sea conditions, which caused the vessel to roll from side to side more than usual. The trawl net then became embedded in the soft seabed, bringing the vessel to a stop in around five seconds. It was the port side of the trawl net which was stuck on the seabed, meaning the *Bugaled Breizh*'s port warp wire (the cable which attaches the trawl net to the ship) would have taken the strain of the snagging and the stern would have been pulled downwards, possibly below the waterline, and large waves would have crashed over the aft deck of the *Bugaled Breizh*. It was likely that the amount of water entering the *Bugaled Breizh* was more than the freeing ports (gaps which allow water to run off the deck) could dispose of, meaning the buoyancy and stability of the *Bugaled Breizh* became compromised. Furthermore, as the hatch to the crew's quarters was in the open position, large amounts of water would have poured into the interior of the ship, further reducing the vessel's stability. The crew made the logical decision to release the port warp wire to relieve the tension, but, as the vessel was still moving forward to pull out of the snag, this would have transferred all of the tension to the starboard warp wire. This would have seen the *Bugaled Breizh* roll over to the starboard side. The water which had built up on the deck and inside the vessel in the crew's quarters would have shifted across to the other side of the ship, causing the *Bugaled Breizh* to capsize and then rapidly sink. The report concluded:

> The interaction between the trawl gear and the sea bottom led
> to a reduction in stability, which was amplified by the sea state
> to such an extent that there was a total loss of stability.

The BEAmer report made immediate safety recommendations. As a matter of urgency, trawlers of a similar type to the *Bugaled Breizh* should keep watertight doors closed at all times, even though it had become common practice for such doors to be secured open when fishing. Further training should be given to trawler crews on how to deal with nets becoming snagged, and changes should also be made in the way radio equipment is used to signal that a vessel is in distress.

Despite the BEAmer report definitively stating that there was no evidence of a submarine causing the sinking, this theory refused to go away. A book entitled *State Secrets Over a Wrecking* by Sebastien Turay and Laurent Richard was published in France in 2007. The authors claimed to have access to confidential NATO documents which showed that HMS *Turbulent* was active in the waters off the coast of Cornwall in the exact area where the *Bugaled Breizh* sank and was not at Devonport Naval Base as the British government and Royal Navy claimed. This led Andrew George, the Liberal Democrat MP for West Cornwall and the Isles of Scilly, to write to the Armed Forces Minister Adam Ingram, asking him to respond to the allegations put forward in the book. Ingram stated that HMS *Turbulent* was in Devonport for the entirety of 15 January, and did not leave until the following day, by which time the *Bugaled Breizh* had already sank. A spokesperson for the MOD told the *Sunday Telegraph* that the claims in *State Secrets over a Wrecking* were "totally unfounded" and were based on a berthing document which was out of date, adding that it was not unusual for such documents to change due to ships and submarine needing unscheduled repairs of maintenance at short notice.

Speculation, Theories and Legal Disputes

With so much speculation over a submarine being involved in the sinking, new theories arose, with multiple submarines being highlighted as being responsible. The Royal Navy submarines HMS *Turbulent* and HMS *Torbay* were identified as possibly being involved in the incident, as were the French nuclear-powered submarine *Rubis*, the German diesel-electric submarine *U-22*, and an unnamed American submarine. It was also speculated that a Russian submarine could have been active in the area to spy on the NATO exercise. This was seen as a particularly feasible theory, as a Russian submarine would have left the area immediately after the collision to avoid detection and made no attempt to rescue survivors or report the sinking of the trawler. However, it was HNLMS *Dolfijn*, which had travelled to the scene to assist in the rescue effort, which drew the most suspicion, with many of the theories stating that the captain of the submarine was willing to help to cover up the fact that it was his submarine which was responsible for the sinking.

In 2009, the French Appeal Court in Nantes, which had previously cleared British and Dutch submarines of involvement, ordered the case to be reopened. An investigator, former French Navy officer Dominique Salles, was tasked with finding out if a submarine did sink the *Bugaled Breizh*, and then, if this was the case, tracing which submarine was responsible. The presence of traces of titanium on the *Bugaled Breizh*'s warp cables was seen as indicative of contact with a submarine, as it was claimed that titanium was found on the hulls of modern submarines.

Many people in both the French and British fishing industries backed the submarine theory and believed that failure to take this claim seriously was putting further fishermen at risk of being capsized by another submarine collision. This was not an unreasonable claim to make as this had indeed happened before. In 1990, four fishermen lost their lives when the Scottish trawler *Antares* sank when the Royal Navy submarine HMS *Trenchant* collided with its nets (this is covered in Chapter Seven of this book).

The families of the *Bugaled Breizh*'s crew had hired lawyers to continue to fight for what they believed was the truth. They remained steadfast in their belief that a submarine was responsible for the loss of the *Bugaled Breizh*, and allegations of a government cover-up continued to grow. A website, SOS *Bugaled Breizh*, was set up. Articles on the site reiterated the claim that titanium was found on the *Bugaled Breizh*'s warp wires, which indicated contact with a submarine, and that as the submarine HNLMS *Dolfijn* was at the scene so quickly it must have been much closer to the *Bugaled Breizh* than previously claimed. They also alleged that the rescue helicopters sent to the scene had sonar domes (indicating they were engaged in a military exercise and not there to search for the *Bugaled Breizh*'s crew) and said, drawing on the claims made by MP Andrew George, that HMS *Turbulent* was not in Devonport but was at sea at the time of the sinking.

However, the families received a succession of significant setbacks from 2013 onward. The Appeal Court of Nantes ended its investigation, which had been led by Dominique Salles, ruling that there had not been any contact between the *Bugaled Breizh*'s nets or warps and a submarine, agreeing with the BEAmer report that the tiny amounts of titanium found on the *Bugaled Breizh* were not consistent with the impact of a submarine. This effectively closed the case, but lawyers representing the families were able to request another hearing at a court in Rennes the following year. At this hearing, the judge agreed that it was unclear why the *Bugaled Breizh* sank but ruled that as there was no evidence that a submarine was involved, there was, therefore, no reason to reopen the case.

This ruling caused fury amongst the families and the wider Breton fishing community. Thierry Lemetayer, son of one of the *Bugaled Breizh*'s crewmembers, was quoted by French news organisation 20 Minutes as saying that the decision of the court was "an insult to the world of fishing and the navy", while Michel Douce, the *Bugaled Breizh*'s owner, spoke of his "anger and rage." Maitre Bergot, a lawyer representing the families said "My clients are tired, tired, disgusted. … It is as if justice had caused the *Bugaled Breizh* to sink a second time and buried the men who were there."

It was announced that the families would appeal to the Court of Cassation, France's highest court for civil and legal matters, to have the decision of the Rennes court overturned. In 2016 the Court of Cassation heard the case and confirmed the decision of the Rennes court, finally and permanently ending any hope of further investigations into the loss of the *Bugaled Breizh* through the French legal system.

British Inquiry

But there was still one option left to the families of the *Bugaled Breizh*'s crew. As the bodies of Yves Gloaguen and Pascal le Floch had been recovered to Cornwall, it was within the power of the British government to carry out an inquest into the deaths of the two men. Such an investigation would be carried out by the Marine Accident Investigation Branch (MAIB) and would cover the entire incident, including investigating the cause of the sinking and, therefore, address the submarine theory once again. It was announced that an inquest and investigation would be held in the UK, although the inquest would be led by a judge, Nigel Lickley QC, and would not be heard by a jury as the families had wanted. Pre-inquest hearings began in 2017, with the full inquest taking place in October 2021. The following month, the findings of the investigation were made public.

Judge Lickley began by stating that everyone who had been called as a witness did their best to assist in the inquiry and highlighted the professionalism and dedication of the people involved in the rescue operation. Leading Aircrewman Darren Hall, who had been lowered from a helicopter to investigate the life raft and recovered two bodies, was singled out for special praise, with Judge Lickley saying that he had risked his life multiple times during the rescue effort. However, Judge Lickley addressed the difficulties in carrying out an inquest more than a decade and a half after the incident, pointing out that people's memories could fade over time. Despite this, he went on to say that the inquiry needed to be held as the families of the dead fishermen had a right to know the truth and it was in the public interest to decisively ascertain what caused the loss of the *Bugaled Breizh*.

Judge Lickley stated that it was within his remit to assess the BEAmer report amid the claims that it was "incomplete, flawed or deficient" and that the findings it reached could not be relied on. He, however, did not find this to be the case and said that the report was "detailed, appropriate, thorough, professional, objective and balanced." He stated that the findings of the British inquiry corroborated much of the BEAmer report, and both investigations reached many of the same conclusions. Collision with a surface vessel, a hard snag with an object on the seabed and catastrophic failure of the *Bugaled Breizh* due to a flaw in its design were all discounted. The long-running submarine theory was also definitively ruled out. The inquiry found that the lack of damage to the trawl nets and warp wires and their position next to the wreck meant no submarine collision had occurred.

The inquiry then systematically listed the submarines in the general area and found that none were near the *Bugaled Breizh* when it sank. *U-22*, the German submarine, was 40 nautical miles (46 miles/74 km) to the east at the time of the sinking and travelling on the surface, and the Royal Navy submarine HMS *Torbay* was 107 nautical miles (123 miles/198 km) away. The positions of both submarines were supported by navigation signals and log book entries. Judge Lickley went on to say that he was satisfied that no submarine was involved in any way with the sinking of *Bugaled Breizh*. HMS *Turbulent*, which had been named in several French investigations, such as the one by the television channel FR3, was at harbour in Devonport and did not depart until 16 January, the day after the *Bugaled Breizh* sank. Navigation signals data and the berthing plan at Devonport backed this up. HMS *Trafalgar* and HMS *Triumph* were also in Devonport and remained there until after the sinking. The French Navy had provided evidence that their nuclear-powered submarine *Rubis* was not involved in the NATO operations that day and was nowhere near the area where the *Bugaled Breizh* sank. Claims that an American or Russian submarine or a civilian-operated submersible may have caused the sinking were "wholly fanciful and unfounded."

The closest submarine to the *Bugaled Breizh* was the Royal Netherlands Navy's HNLMS *Dolfijn*. It was at least 11 nautical miles (12 miles/20 km) away when the *Bugaled Breizh* sank. Judge Lickley accepted that the presence of a surfaced submarine taking part in a search and rescue operation was highly unusual and may have been the cause of the claims that a submarine was responsible for the sinking. Still, he was satisfied that this was not the case and reiterated that HNLMS *Dolfijn* was in the area to assist with the search and for no other reason. The claim that HNLMS *Dolfijn* had been "evading" vessels such as the *Eridan* during the search was also rejected by the inquiry. Judge Lickley stated that HNLMS *Dolfijn* had made its location known to Falmouth MRCC in Cornwall and had also been in radio contact with the skipper of the British fishing boat *Silver Dawn* to ensure that the two vessels remained a safe distance apart while they were searching for survivors.

He went on to say that he saw no evidence of any kind of cover-up or misdirection from the Royal Navy or British government. The Royal Navy officers who had provided evidence to the inquiry, Rear Admiral Simon Asquith, Commander Daniel Simmonds and Commander Andrew Coles, were described as being "credible" and "accurate" with their information on submarine movements, and this information was corroborated by other sources such as berthing plans, submarine logs and navigation signals. Captain Van Driel and Captain Van Zanten of the Royal Netherlands Navy, who provided information on the *Dolfijn*'s movements were also praised for the quality of the evidence they provided.

Ultimately, the inquiry concurred with the BEAmer report. Judge Lickley stated that a soft snag of the trawl nets on the seabed was the decisive factor which caused the loss of the *Bugaled Breizh*. But a soft snag alone was not enough to cause the sinking and he agreed the downflooding of water into the crew's quarters, and the shifting of this water from one side of the vessel to the other when the warp wires were released, were the additional factors which caused *Bugaled Breizh* to capsize. The official cause of death of Pascal Le Floch and Yves Gloaguen was recorded as drowning following the accidental sinking of the *Bugaled Breizh*.

But at least some evidence uncovered in the inquiry supported the cover-up claims. Peter McLelland had been a captain in the Royal Marines (he was retired by the time of the inquiry) and was the pilot of the Sea King helicopter which recovered the bodies of Pascal Le Floch and Yves Gloaguen. He told the inquiry that when he returned to base and attended a debrief, his commanding officer told him not to mention that he had seen a submarine (HNLMS *Dolfijn*) in the area where the *Bugaled Breizh* sank. In an official report, which was completed after a search and rescue operation as a matter of routine, there was no mention of a submarine being present during the search for survivors. No reason was given for failing to mention the submarine, and when the commanding officer was questioned, he said that he could not remember giving the debrief but believed it was the responsibility of the captain of HMS *Tyne* (which had taken responsibility for coordinating the rescue operation) to report the presence of the submarine.

End of Legal Action and Dismantling of the Wreck

Through the BEAmer report and the UK's MAIB inquiry, two official investigations had reached the same conclusion – the *Bugaled Breizh* sank when its trawl gear encountered a soft snag on the seabed. Both investigations also ruled out a collision with a ship, a hard snag on the seabed or a design or construction flaw as causing the loss of the vessel, and both had eliminated the involvement of a submarine. With their legal options in the French courts exhausted and the British inquiry confirming the findings of the BEAmer report, there was now no possibility of the lawyers representing the families of the *Bugaled Breizh*'s crew to force any further investigations into the loss of the vessel. Many people within the Brittany fishing community still feel anger and resentment over the investigations into the *Bugaled Breizh* to this day and continue to believe that the true reason for the sinking has not come to light. Family members of the men who lost their lives on the *Bugaled Breizh* continue to fight for further investigations to be carried out and remain steadfast in their belief that a submarine played a pivotal role in the loss of the vessel.

The wreck of the *Bugaled Breizh* had been securely stored at Brest Arsenal since its refloating in 2004. It was maintained during the ongoing legal appeals as it might have needed to be examined again in a future investigation. But with legal proceedings in both Britain and France concluded, the French Court of Appeal in Rennes ordered the wreck to be dismantled. A group of around twenty family members and the vessel's owner Michel Douce attended a private ceremony to say a final farewell to the *Bugaled Breizh* in April 2023 before the wreck was removed for dismantling. Memorials to the crew of the *Bugaled Breizh* have been built in both Brittany and Cornwall.

The *Bugaled Breizh* remains in the public consciousness in France as evidenced by the level of media attention still dedicated to uncovering the truth about the vessel. As of early 2024, the website SOS *Bugaled Breizh* remains online, and in 2016, a graphic novel, *37 Seconds*, was published. Written by Pascal Bresson and Erwan Le Saec, its name was taken from the amount of time it was calculated the *Bugaled Breizh* took to sink. A documentary film about the loss of the *Bugaled Breizh* created by Jacques Losay, the father-in-law of the *Bugaled Breizh*'s captain Yves Gloaguen, was also released in 2013. In 2022, the music streaming service Spotify released a six-part investigative podcast, *En Eaux Troubles* (*In Troubled Waters*). Spotify says that the podcast "reopen[s] this case and point[s] out the inconsistencies of an expert report … on which the judges relied to render their decision to dismiss the case."

Chapter 5

The *Pelican*

The *Pelican* was a recreational fishing boat which operated out of Montauk in Long Island, New York State. On the morning of 1 September 1951, the *Pelican* set off for the Frisbie Bank fishing grounds with more than sixty people on board. But the pleasant weather of the morning would soon worsen, and by the end of the day, forty-five people on board the *Pelican* would be either dead or missing.

Montauk is an island located at the eastern tip of Long Island in New York State, although many refer to it as a peninsula due to the many bridges connecting it to the mainland. Its location, jutting out into the Atlantic Ocean, means it had long been a hub of commercial fishing with trawlers catching species such as herring, mackerel, flounder, monkfish, tuna and cod. But from the 1920s onwards, growing numbers of recreational anglers were attracted to the area by the number and size of fish that could be caught relatively close to shore. In the early days of Montauk's recreational fishing boom, anglers would ask the captains of commercial fishing boats if they could pay for a place on board and fish with a rod and line from the stern of trawlers. Many trawler captains allowed this, seeing it as an easy way to make additional revenue, but soon, enterprising captains worked out that more money could be made by switching from commercial fishing to catering for anglers, and Montauk's recreational fishing industry began to grow.

Recreational Angling in Montauk

By the early 1950s, recreational fishing was hugely popular in Montauk, with the most successful captains making a lucrative income from their boats. Two types of angling boats had become established. Charter boats typically left early in the morning, carrying no more than six anglers who had pre-booked their place on the boat and were happy to pay a higher price for a serious fishing experience led by a captain who knew how to locate the largest fish, such as marlin, swordfish, tuna or sharks. The other type of boat was known as an open boat. This was because such boats were open to all – anglers did not book a place in advance and instead simply turned up and bought a ticket as they walked on board, with places allocated on a first-come, first-served basis. Open boats attracted a less serious type of angler, and some people on board did not even take part in fishing, instead being happy to drink beer or soft drinks, chat with other passengers, sunbathe and listen to music while on board. For this reason, these open boats were also known as party boats. A train, known as the Fisherman's Special, would bring crowds of people from New York City to Montauk in the mid-morning, releasing them just a few hundred metres from the fishing piers where the open boats were based. At weekends and public holidays, there would be many more people wanting to go out on open boats than there were places available. This resulted in a manic rush as the Fisherman's Special trains opened their doors and crowds of people carrying fishing rods, tackle boxes, coolers full of beer and lunches in brown paper bags descended on the open boats, all desperate to secure their place.

The *Pelican* operated as an open boat. It was constructed in Brooklyn in 1940, was 13 metres (42 ft) long, and had a gross tonnage of 14 tons. Originally named *Bell Boy III*, it was purchased by 34-year-old Edward Carroll in 1950, who immediately renamed it the *Pelican* and based it at Fishangri-la Pier at Montauk. Carroll had extensive seafaring experience, having served as a yacht captain, crewmember of a cargo vessel and as a non-commissioned officer in the Pacific Theatre during the Second

World War. But it was as an open boat captain where Carroll excelled. He was well-liked by his fellow fishing boat captains and had an excellent reputation for looking after his passengers and ensuring they caught plenty of fish.

The gross tonnage of the *Pelican* was significant. Regulations at the time stated that vessels with a gross tonnage of more than 15 tons required annual Coast Guard safety inspections and limits on the number of passengers they carried. As the *Pelican* had been specifically designed to have a gross tonnage of 14 tons, there were remarkably few regulations to which the vessel had to adhere. Indeed, the only two major regulations were that it had to be issued with a permanent licence by the US Collector of Customs in New York and have enough lifejackets for everyone on board every time it went to sea. Carroll had received the permanent licence in May of 1950 and two metal lockers on board the *Pelican* held around eighty lifejackets, meaning that Carroll was adhering to the laws and regulations in place at that time. Furthermore, Carroll had invested significant funds in buying the *Pelican* and had maintained the vessel well, having both of the 100 horsepower Chrysler engines overhauled at a cost of $3,000 in 1951 – the equivalent of more than $30,000 (approximately £23,500) in 2024.

Edward Carroll and Robert Scanlon

The *Pelican* operated with a crew of two. Carroll was both the owner and captain of the vessel, and as well as his extensive maritime experience, he also possessed a Motorboat Operator's Licence, meaning he was fully qualified for the role. The same could not be said of the other crewmember, the mate, Robert Scanlon. Aged twenty-three, he had no maritime experience before being employed by Carroll and had no licence or other seafaring credentials, although the lack of regulations for boats with a gross tonnage of 14 tons or under meant that he was not required to have any qualifications. Indeed, Scanlon only worked on board the *Pelican* on a part-time basis during the busy summer months and maintained other employment as a short-order cook in the winter. Still, Scanlon had proved adequate as a mate on the *Pelican*, and many other open and charter boat captains employed their inexperienced and unqualified sons in the same role, and the majority of them were much younger than Scanlon.

The Final Voyage of the *Pelican*

Saturday 1 September 1951 was the first day of the Labor Day Weekend, a federal holiday which celebrates and recognises the workers who helped build the United States. This, along with the good weather and the productivity of late summer fishing, meant that it would be an exceptionally busy day for both the charter and open boats. From 6.00 am, the charter boats left the sheltered waters of the piers, rounded Montauk Lighthouse, and sailed out into the open waters of the Atlantic Ocean. A few hours later, the Fisherman's Special trains arrived, and hundreds of people rushed to secure their place on board an open boat. Many made their way to Carroll and the *Pelican*, and the boat soon began to fill up. People pushed and jostled for a place on the boat and Robert Scanlon, who had been tasked with selling tickets to people as they walked on board, struggled to keep up. Based on the ticket stubs it would appear that fifty-four people were on board the *Pelican* that day, although it would later emerge that more people had been let on board – possibly because Carroll did not want to let down regular customers and found a space for them – bringing the total, including the two crew, to sixty-four.

At 8.30 am, the *Pelican*, low in the waterline and moving slower than usual due to the number of people on board, made its way around the lighthouse and out into the Atlantic. Carroll was taking his boat to a popular fishing area known as Frisbie Bank, eleven miles out to sea. Once it was out into the open ocean, the *Pelican* was propelled by the wind and tide, meaning it made good time, arriving at Frisbie Bank at 10.00 am. The engines were cut, hooks were baited, and lines lowered into the water.

Radios were switched on, and music could be heard across the *Pelican* while the coolers containing beer were opened, and people began drinking and fishing. The fishing was slow to begin with, but Carroll rejected calls to move to a new spot after such a short amount of time. It was the right decision to make, and soon, people started catching porgy (a species of sea bream) and seabass. All appeared well on board the *Pelican*, but above the boat, the first grey clouds were beginning to appear.

No fishing boat captains wanted to cut short a day's fishing unnecessarily due to bad weather, and the consensus was always to wait and see how the weather conditions developed and head back to port only if it was absolutely necessary. There was no official policy on refunds if boats had to return early. Some captains would issue half refunds if their passengers only got half a day's fishing, although most resisted doing this if they could, pointing out to anglers that it cost them the same in fuel to head out and come back regardless of how much time was spent fishing. By 10.30 am, all of the fishing boat captains who were at sea that day were growing increasingly concerned about the changing weather conditions. As the wind grew stronger and the size of the waves began to increase, the first boats turned to head back to Montauk. Edward Carroll's brother, Howard, was also a fishing boat captain who had also taken passengers out that day. He radioed Edward and told him he was taking his boat, *Jigger II*, back due to the worsening weather and suggested Edward do the same. According to the official report into the disaster, Edward replied "We're getting a few fish, it's pretty good down here" and said that he would stay out a little longer. While Howard was concerned, he respected his brother's knowledge and ability to read the weather and sea conditions. Howard Carroll turned the *Jigger II* back to Montauk, leaving Edward and the *Pelican* fishing at Frisbie Bank.

Just fifteen minutes later, Edward Carroll gave the call for all lines to be reeled in and announced that they were heading back to Montauk. While this led to complaints from some of the anglers, others were keen to return. The sea had been turning increasingly choppy, causing the *Pelican* to roll from side to side which made some of the passengers feel seasick, while others had become concerned about the clouds which had turned from grey to black and were beginning to fill the sky and the wind which was now starting to whip up spray off the surface of the sea. Unknown to Carroll, a trawler fishing much further out in the Atlantic had radioed to the Coast Guard station to inform them that a ferocious storm was closing in with great speed and would soon reach Montauk. Furthermore, just as the *Pelican* arrived at Frisbie Bank, an updated weather forecast had been circulated across ports and harbours in the region, warning of rapidly worsening conditions and advising fishing boats to remain in port. While the dock staff at Fishangri-la Pier had received this updated report, it was not radioed to charter or open boat captains on the basis that they would not cut a day's fishing short due to a weather forecast which may prove to be inaccurate, and they were more than capable of reading the weather conditions and deciding when to come in themselves.

Attempt to Return to Montauk

As the *Pelican*'s engines were started for the return journey, the port engine spluttered and then cut out. Carroll and Scanlon spent ten minutes trying to restart the engine but were unsuccessful, leaving Carroll with no choice other than to head back on one engine. The *Pelican* began to move painfully slowly back toward Fishangri-la Pier, now not only down to one engine but also sailing against the wind and tide. Rain began to come down heavily, and the covered section of the boat soon filled up with passengers seeking shelter, but the vast majority had to stay out at their fishing positions along the sides of the boat. Many set their fishing rods to one side and used both hands to hang on to the railings as the rising and falling seas began to rock the *Pelican* violently up and down. Waves, some of which reached 2 metres (6 ft) in height struck the *Pelican* as it struggled to make its way back home, travelling at a speed of just two or three knots (around 3 mph).

In the book *Dark Noon*, Tom Clavin describes the deteriorating weather conditions and the impact this had on Carroll and his passengers. Carroll was up on the bridge, exposed to the worst of the storm, straining to steer and manoeuvre the *Pelican* as best he could as waves crashed over him and the wind whipped stinging spray off the sea. Below him, passengers clung on to anything they could. Clavin writes that the "Lucky or smart ones stayed where they could see the waves coming and thus had a couple of seconds to brace themselves before each impact" but others who were too "wet and cold, or tired and frightened to care" simply allowed themselves to be buffeted and battered by the incoming waves. Clavin writes that Carroll remained confident that he would make it back safely, even if the journey would take two and a half hours and would be extremely uncomfortable. He states that Carroll thought that it would be close, but they would just make it back in time. The journey back would later be something they could laugh about over a drink in a bar back in Montauk, and the passengers would have a "good story to tell their grandchildren."

By 1.30 pm the berths at Fishangri-la Pier were starting to fill up with returning fishing boats. While it was noted that the *Pelican* had still not returned, no one was overly concerned as a few other fishing boats still had not arrived and there was still time for the *Pelican* to return before the storm fully closed in. Howard Carroll had safely sailed *Jigger II* back to Fishangri-la and tried to contact Edward by radio. He became increasingly worried when he received no response but convinced himself that Edward might have his hands full sailing the *Pelican* through the rough seas, meaning he could not answer, or the radio may have become inoperable through being covered by rain or seawater during the storm.

As Howard was trying to contact Edward, the *Pelican* was within one mile of Montauk Lighthouse, and safety was in sight. This was, paradoxically, the most dangerous part of the journey back. The unique conditions of Montauk Point created a riptide where a strong offshore counter-current would have to be sailed through to gain access to the harbour. As this was negotiated, the starboard side of the *Pelican* would be fully exposed to the waves from the open sea. In calm weather this was a difficult task, but in storm conditions and only a single engine working, it would be highly dangerous.

The waves reached heights of 3.5 metres (12 ft) as the *Pelican* approached the riptide, but its single engine could not generate enough power to progress – the counter-current was taking the *Pelican* backwards at the same speed the engine drove it forward. Effectively stuck, and with its starboard side exposed to the full force of the storm, the *Pelican* was rocked by a huge wave but managed to right itself. But seconds later, another wave, later estimated to be between 4.5 and 6 metres (15 and 20 ft) high by survivors, slammed into the side of the *Pelican* and capsized the boat.

Passengers were thrown into the sea. Some grasped lifejackets and wooden fishing tackle boxes which had been thrown from the boat as it overturned; others managed to swim toward the upturned hull of the *Pelican* and cling on, but others, weighed down by clothing and boots were only able to tread water for a short amount of time before coldness and exhaustion became too much for them and they sank beneath the waves. Some passengers, who had been sheltering within the covered cabin of the *Pelican* when it capsized, were trapped inside the vessel. While there would have been an air pocket inside the cabin, it is unknown how long those stuck inside the inverted *Pelican* lived, and no one trapped in this position survived.

Only one person – a passenger named John Griffin – had donned a lifejacket at the start of the journey. While he was heavily mocked for this by fellow passengers, he would be one of the survivors. A few other passengers had put lifejackets on when they realised the *Pelican* was in trouble, but at no point during the attempted journey back to Montauk did Carroll or Scanlon order any of the passengers to put on a lifejacket. This may have been because they thought giving such an order would have caused more fear and panic among the passengers, or they may have simply forgotten to issue such an instruction even though the *Pelican*, even in its overloaded state, had a plentiful supply of lifejackets – more than enough for everyone on board.

While Carroll tried his best to coordinate some sort of order from his position on the upturned hull, the situation was chaotic, with people crying out and screaming for help. Approximately twenty people clung to the hull, but this number was reduced with each successive wave which washed over the *Pelican* sweeping people away. To make matters worse, the *Pelican* was also sinking, with the amount of the vessel protruding out of the water progressively reducing as time passed, leaving less and less of the hull for survivors to hold onto.

Rescue Attempts

Suddenly, a private fishing boat, the *Betty Anne*, arrived on the scene. Captained by naval reservist Harold R. Bishop, the *Betty Anne* was also returning to Montauk, like the *Pelican* trying to outrun the storm. Bishop stopped his boat, threw lifejackets into the water and then used ropes to drag survivors into the *Betty Anne*. But the conditions were treacherous, with huge waves crashing across the bow of the *Betty Anne*, and Bishop was worried that he too might be capsized. Despite this, he continued to try to rescue survivors. A short while later, the charter boat *Bingo II*, captained by Lester Behan, a member of the United States Coast Guard Auxiliary, made its way to the scene and also began rescuing survivors from the water, although the crew soon realised that most of the people they dragged on board were already dead.

In the official report into the disaster, it was stated that Bishop was limited as to how many people he could rescue as other than him, the only other people on board the *Betty Anne* were too old, frail or young to help. The report outlines the other challenges which faced both the *Betty Anne* and the *Bingo II*. The storm conditions made the sea incredibly rough, and the two boats had to manoeuvre between people swimming and treading water. Ropes and lines from the *Pelican* crisscrossed the surface and threatened to foul the propellors of the rescuing boats. Even when survivors were located, most had no energy or strength to help themselves on board, making it difficult for the rescuers to get people onto the boats.

After twenty to twenty-five minutes in the area, Bishop and Behan believed that they could see no further survivors in the water, and, growing concerned that some of the people they had rescued may die if they did not soon receive medical attention, both vessels headed back to Montauk. The *Betty Anne* had successfully rescued six people from the water, and twelve more survivors were on board the *Bingo II*. In the book *Dark Noon*, Tom Clavin writes that Behan and other crewmembers on board *Bingo II* saw Edward Carroll alive in the water, helping survivors toward the two boats. He refused to be brought on board *Bingo II* and stayed in the water to continue assisting survivors. Behan and crewmembers of the *Bingo II* watched as a series of large waves swamped the area, and Carroll disappeared beneath the surface. His body was never recovered. As the *Betty Anne* and *Bingo II* sailed back to Montauk, heavy waves continued to strike the upturned hull of the *Pelican*, which began to sink further beneath the water until it was barely visible.

Back in Montauk, charter and open boat captains were now highly concerned about the absence of the *Pelican*. Howard Carroll had made numerous further attempts to contact his brother on the radio. He stood out on the piers during the storm, wanting to be the first to see the *Pelican* round the lighthouse and return to the harbour. But it was Archie Jones, a coastguard staff member stationed in Montauk lighthouse, who confirmed Howard Carroll's worst fears. He had seen the *Pelican* battle against the riptide from his vantage point in the lighthouse. But he had no way of knowing how serious the situation was, being unaware that the *Pelican* was overloaded with passengers and struggling with only one functioning engine. To Jones, the *Pelican* was fully capable of rounding the lighthouse and returning to Fishangri-la Pier in the same way as all of the other boats had. This meant that he did not raise the alarm until he saw the *Pelican* capsize.

It took only minutes for news of the *Pelican*'s capsizing to spread through the Montauk fishing community. Preparations were immediately made to receive the casualties, with the ballroom of Montauk Yacht Club being rapidly transformed into a treatment room as people arrived with blankets, food, and medical supplies. Police and fire engines arrived at Montauk, followed by ambulances and doctors and nurses from nearby hospitals and members of the public made their way to the area to help in any way they could. The ice house at the port, usually used to hold the catches of fish unloaded from commercial vessels, was converted into a makeshift morgue.

Fellow fishing boat captains went to their boats and bravely headed back out into the storm, making for the location of the *Pelican*. Two of the first to set out were *Viking V*, captained by Carl Fosberg, and *Cricket II*, captained by Frank Mundus. While Mundus was, at this point, a little-known open boat captain, building up his reputation following his move to Montauk from New Jersey, he would go on to become extremely famous through his fishing exploits. In his later charter boat career, he would pioneer the targeting of large sharks, becoming one of the most successful proponents of this type of fishing, catching a 3,247lb (1,472kg) great white shark on rod and line less than thirty miles off Montauk Point in the 1980s. Mundus is widely believed to be the inspiration for the character Quint in the 1975 film *Jaws*.

The Coast Guard response was confused and muddled. On hearing of the emergency, Coast Guard officials in New York discussed which vessels to send with their counterparts in Boston, seemingly oblivious to the urgency of the situation. After much deliberation, the powerful and well-equipped 25 metre (83 ft) long Coast Guard cutter *Tamaroa* was eventually dispatched to take part in the rescue effort. Leaving the seaport in New London, Connecticut it was at Montauk within an hour. But instead of proceeding to the scene of the disaster, the *Tamaroa* inexplicably docked in Lake Montauk at the end of the peninsula. The crew claimed that they could not sail to the *Pelican* until they had direct orders to do so. As the much smaller Montauk Coast Guard vessels and fishing boats headed back out into the storm, the *Tamaroa* remained in Lake Montauk, much to the distress and anger of fishermen and family members of those on the *Pelican*. Even when the anger boiled over and people began shouting at the crew of the *Tamaroa* and throwing rocks at the vessel, it did not move and never left Lake Montauk to assist with the rescue effort.

The only Coast Guard vessels which would, therefore, take part in the rescue operation were the small motor lifeboats stationed at Montauk. Despite Montauk's popularity as a recreational and commercial fishing destination, there were only three rescue vessels to cover the whole area, all of which were built in the 1920s and were between 7.5 and 10.5 metres (25 - 35 ft) in length. With the Korean War going on at the time of the disaster, there was no money available to upgrade or replace Coast Guard vessels, and the number of Coast Guard staff stationed at Montauk had been significantly reduced in the years leading up to 1951. As Tom Clavin stated in *Dark Noon* the "line of defence against tragedy in Montauk waters was stretched dangerously thin."

One of the Montauk Coast Guard boats was captained by Purnell Curles, the Officer in Charge of the Ditch Plain Coast Guard station at Montauk. But he would take over an hour to arrive at the scene of the *Pelican*, having been in Napeague Bay on the inland side of the peninsula, responding to what turned out to be a false alarm of a small boat in trouble, when word of the *Pelican* reached him. The first Coast Guard officer to arrive at the *Pelican* was Kenneth R. Whiting. He had received the call that the *Pelican* was in trouble and immediately drove to Montauk Harbour and readied the Coast Guard picket boat *CG 38523* (a type of small patrol boat) to head out to rescue survivors. By the time he reached the *Pelican*, it was 15.15 pm, several hours after the capsizing, and the *Pelican* had almost completely sunk beneath the water. But as Whiting drew closer, he saw that a single person was still clinging to the tiny part of the hull which remained above the waterline. Antonio Borruso climbed aboard the picket boat and became the nineteenth and final survivor rescued from the *Pelican*.

Recovery of the *Pelican*

Soon afterwards Frank Mundus in *Cricket II* and Carl Fosberg in *Viking V*, along with a few additional crew members in each boat, arrived at the *Pelican*, which was almost completely submerged. While the storm had abated, the sea was still extremely rough, with large waves crashing against their boats. At great risk to their own safety, they decided to recover the wreck of the *Pelican*, believing there was a small chance that people could still be alive, trapped inside the *Pelican*. Even if there were no survivors, they believed that there were likely to still be bodies on board and they could be recovered if the vessel was saved from sinking to the seabed. They managed to manoeuvre their boats close enough to the wreck to attach ropes and began to make the slow and dangerous journey back to port, towing the sinking wreck of the *Pelican* behind them.

For six hours the *Cricket II* and *Viking V* slowly dragged the *Pelican* back toward Montauk. While the storm's strength had reduced considerably, the seas were still rough, and they moved at a speed of just a few knots as they fought against the wind and tide. Frank Mundus died at the age of eighty-two in 2008, but as of 2024, his personal website is still online, although it has not been updated since his death. On the page entitled *PELICAN* DISASTER, SEPT. 1 1951, he explains that as he and Captain Fosberg reached Montauk Point, and had almost completed the journey back, a large Coast Guard cutter which had sailed to the area from Connecticut approached them. The Coast Guard vessel wanted to take over towing the *Pelican* but Mundus and Fosberg refused, wanting to complete the journey themselves. After something of a stand-off, the towing of the *Pelican* was handed over to the Coast Guard vessel. On his website, Mundus wrote:

> In the newspapers, the Coast Guard got all the glory. Forsberg and I got no recognition at all for doing all this work. The only thing we wanted from the Press was one word: "Thanks," but never got it.

Eventually, the Coast Guard cutter towing the almost entirely submerged *Pelican* arrived at port in Montauk in the early hours of Sunday 2 September. Still in an inverted position, the *Pelican* was secured alongside a trawler, and divers were sent to search the wreck for anyone who may have survived inside an air pocket in the vessel. Several bodies were found, but no survivors were present, with the divers remarking that it looked as if many of the people had become crushed as they all tried to force their way out of the upturned cabin of the *Pelican* at the same time. By the Sunday morning, the families of the passengers on board the *Pelican* began to arrive in Montauk, desperate for news of their loved ones. Some were reunited with those who had survived the disaster while others had to identify their dead family members in the makeshift ice house morgue. Some families desperately searched for news of missing people, not knowing if they had boarded the *Pelican* the previous morning or had chosen to do something else that day and were elsewhere in Montauk, safe and well. A definitive list of those who died in the disaster, or were still missing, would not be compiled for several weeks, as no one knew exactly how many people had been on board the *Pelican* when it capsized. In the following month, bodies from the *Pelican* kept on washing up on beaches or being discovered by commercial and recreational fishermen out at sea, meaning that the number of people who lost their lives in the disaster was constantly being revised upward. No fishing boats left Montauk the day after the disaster. Although anglers turned up looking to go fishing, the sea conditions, which were still rough due to the remnants of the storm, were used as the reason to keep all of the boats in port.

Investigation, Legislation and the Fate of the *Pelican*

On 7 September, a week after the disaster, the wreck of the *Pelican* was inspected by the US Marine Board of Investigation. Their initial findings were that other than the faulty engine, the vessel was in good condition, and there was no evidence of any structural damage before the capsizing. They continued their investigation and published their official report into the loss of the *Pelican* on 8 October 1951. The report blamed Edward Carroll for the excessive number of passengers he admitted on board the

Pelican. This was identified as the decisive cause of the disaster, and any additional factors played little role in the loss. The report stated:

> Wind and sea conditions, failure to distribute passenger weight to the best advantage, and uncertain engine operation – were purely accessory and would have had no serious effect if the primary, governing cause – overloading – had not existed.

The report went on to say if the *Pelican*'s gross tonnage was one ton greater, it would have needed to be inspected and certified by the Coast Guard. If such an inspection had taken place, the *Pelican* would not have been permitted to carry more than twenty passengers. They also said that if Edward Carroll had been alive and able to defend himself he would have been subject to serious criminal charges. The report also finally stated the number of casualties in the disaster. Nineteen people, including the mate Robert Scanlon, had survived, twenty-six were confirmed dead, and nineteen were missing, one of which was Edward Carroll. Later, all of the missing people would be declared dead, bringing the total to forty-five.

It did not take long for fishing to return to Montauk. Less than two weeks later local newspapers reported that cod and bass were being caught in good numbers and there was much celebration when a tuna of close to 1,000lb was landed on the boat *Scamp II* at the end of September. But reports from the time also stated that the number of people opting to fish from open boats was significantly reduced following the *Pelican* disaster, with those who continued fishing mostly choosing to fish from charter boats instead.

In the following years, the families of those who died and several survivors took legal action against the estate of Edward Carroll and the company which ran the Fishangri-la Pier from which the *Pelican* departed, seeking $1.7 million in damages (the equivalent of around $25 million in 2024). A total of eleven lawsuits were put forward, but the estate of Edward Carroll was later removed from the litigation when it emerged that its only assets were an engagement ring and the wreck of the *Pelican*.

When a test case, brought by the wife of one of those who lost their lives on board the *Pelican*, was thrown out by a judge, the other lawsuits were all refused, meaning that legally, no one was ever held responsible for the disaster.

The regulations governing party and open boats with tonnages of 14 tons and under were eventually changed, although the legislation to enact this was not implemented until 1956. The new legislation meant that boats of any tonnage which were 20 metres (65 ft) in length or greater now had to limit the number of people on board, carry lifesaving equipment, and all crew members had to be properly qualified. The legislation was estimated to apply to around 8,000 boats across the country.

The *Pelican* suffered an ignominious fate. Tom Clavin explains that the vessel was put into a dry dock in Greenport, Long Island where it languished, becoming mostly forgotten as time passed. As the decades went by, the *Pelican* deteriorated in condition as the elements took their toll on the vessel, and later years saw it become something of a local attraction for young people who smoked and drank inside its hull which was also vandalised and covered in graffiti. In the 1990s, the dry dock complex was sold to a housing developer but was not immediately demolished. Instead, the dry dock was deliberately set on fire as part of a training exercise for the Greenport Fire Department, with the *Pelican* going up in flames with the rest of the buildings.

Chapter 6

The Morecambe Bay Cockling Disaster

In 2004, a group of Chinese workers who had been illegally trafficked to the UK were tasked with picking cockles in Morecambe Bay. Untrained, inexperienced and speaking little English, the group were unaware of the dangers the area posed and continued working until they were surrounded by the incoming tide. It would soon emerge that at least twenty-one of the cockle pickers lost their lives that night on the sands of Morecambe Bay.

Morecambe Bay is a large, natural bay in Lancashire in northwest England. Covering close to 310 square kilometres (200 sq. miles), it is the second largest bay in the United Kingdom after the Wash. It takes its name from the nearby town and seaside resort of Morecambe. While the bay is vast and sandy, it is also very dangerous. The bay has a very high tidal range – the difference between the high and low tide water levels. The lowest tides, as measured on the local scale, are just one metre (3 ft), but high tides can measure 10.5 metres (35 ft). The distance between the high and low tide points is correspondingly large and can measure more than 7.5 miles (12 km) on the biggest tides. Morecambe Bay's funnel-like shape creates areas of strong tidal flow along channels, some of which can be more than 10 metres (32 ft) deep. The ground of the bay is made up of a mix of sand, saltmarsh and mudflats, with many areas being soft and silty, creating a quicksand effect in many parts of the bay. Across much of the bay, the tide can come in much faster than a person can return to the safety of the shoreline. Indeed, the bay is so dangerous that an official Guide to the Sands has been appointed by the King or Queen since 1548. Cedric Robinson served as the Guide to the Sands between 1963 and 2019, helping an estimated half a million people safely cross Morecambe Bay. Following his retirement, local fisherman Michael Wilson took over the role.

Cockle Picking in Morecambe Bay

A wide variety of fish are found in and around Morecambe Bay, with flatfish such as plaice, dab and flounder present, along with bass, silver eels, cod and whiting supporting a commercial fishing industry in the area. However, Morecambe Bay also has valuable shellfish beds. Cockles – an edible species of saltwater clam – have historically been one of the most important shellfish found in Morecambe Bay. They are widely eaten in the UK and are traditionally sold by the pint or half pint in fishmongers, although many of the cockles gathered in the UK are now exported. Cockles bury themselves in the sand in the intertidal zone and filter-feed on small pieces of organic matter suspended in the water. They can grow to a maximum size of 6 centimetres (2 ins) across the shell. Cockles can be gathered in several ways. Fishing boats can tow a mechanical dredge to collect cockles from the seabed, or a suction dredge which uses powerful jets of water to remove cockles from the sediment can also be used. But venturing out to the low tide line to collect cockles with simple tools (such as rakes) or simply by hand has been practised in Morecambe Bay for generations and continues to this day.

The Chinese immigrants who lost their lives in the cockle picking disaster had arrived in Britain in the preceding months, with most thought to have arrived illegally in shipping containers at the Port of Liverpool. The majority came from the Fukien Province, one of China's poorest regions, and had paid thousands of pounds to gangmasters (known as 'snakeheads') who arranged the trafficking of the immigrants from China to Britain. Lin Liang Ren, a Chinese national who was based in Liverpool, was heavily involved in trafficking immigrants into the UK. He oversaw around seventy Chinese illegal immigrants who lived in just four houses in Liverpool and Morecambe, with as many as eight people sleeping on mattresses on the floor of each room. Many of the Chinese immigrants had taken on debt to fund the journey to Britain but were told that they could make as much as 10,000 yuan (£715) a month – a good salary in China. This would allow them to quickly pay off their debt to the gangmasters and begin making money for themselves and to send to their families. The reality was that they were used to carry out a range of menial, low-skilled work, for which they would be paid a fraction of the UK minimum wage, allowing Lin Liang Ren to make vast profits from their labour and leaving them little chance of ever paying off their debts.

The Incoming Tide

On 5 February 2004, a group of between thirty and forty Chinese immigrants, aged between 18 and 45, were taken to Morecambe Bay by Lin Liang Ren to pick cockles. They were mostly from rural areas of Fukien Province, spoke little to no English, and had not received any training or been provided with any safety equipment. At low tide, they walked across the flat, wet sands of the bay to an area known as Warton Sands. The area had previously been closed to cockle pickers due to its dangerous location but was reopened in 2003 by the North Wales and North West Sea Fisheries Committee on the basis that shellfish could be collected safely there by people with full knowledge of the area and an awareness of the tides. As shellfish had not been collected over the previous years when the area was closed, Warton Sands were abundant with cockles. Lin Liang Ren had made no attempt to warn the group how dangerous Morecambe Bay was, and all the Chinese workers were oblivious to the danger of the incoming tide. Each cockle picker was reportedly paid £5 for each 25 kg (55 lb) bag of cockles they gathered, although a report from the *Independent* newspaper at the time of the disaster claimed that each worker was paid £1 for a nine-hour shift.

At 4.00 pm, they arrived at the site and began work, picking cockles from the sediment by hand. While Lin Liang Ren had led the workers there, he did not stay with them and returned to the shoreline to wait in a van. A small group of local cockle pickers working nearby approached the Chinese group and tried to tell them that they must leave the area as the weather conditions were deteriorating, and there was only a short time left before the tide began to come in. Due to the language barrier, communication with the Chinese group was difficult, and the local cockle pickers resorted to tapping their watches to try and convey that there was not much time left. However, the Chinese cockle pickers either ignored or did not understand the attempts to warn them of the dangers, and the Coast Guard was not informed that people were staying out on a dangerous part of the bay as the tide came in.

The Chinese cockle pickers continued to work for the next few hours, unaware that the incoming tide had already cut them off, and they were effectively trapped on an island of sand which was rapidly decreasing in size as the water continued to race in around them. At around 9.30 pm, the group realised they were in trouble and began to try to make their way back to shore. Fourteen of the cockle pickers, employing a mix of wading and swimming through the water, managed to escape the tide and reach the safety of the shoreline. But many others drowned or died from the effects of hypothermia while trying to reach safety. Some had used their mobile phones to call family members back in China and say their final goodbyes as the waters rose around them and they realised that they were going to die. One man managed to phone the emergency services but, due to his lack of English, was only able to repeat the phrase "sinking water" and could not explain where he was or what was happening. The operator who took the call later reported that she could hear the sound of high winds, splashing water and the crying and shouting of people in distress in the background as the man spoke.

As the survivors collapsed exhausted back on the shore, Lin Liang Ren realised what had happened. But it would later emerge that he waited almost an hour before phoning 999 and informing the authorities that people were lost out on the bay. When the police, ambulances and coastguard did arrive, Lin Liang Ren and his associates, which included his girlfriend, Zhao Xiao Qing, and his cousin, Lin Mu Yong, intermixed with the survivors and pretended that they had also been out cockle picking on the sands.

The Search and Rescue Operation

Eventually, a large-scale search and rescue operation was put into action involving the coastguard, lifeboat crews, hovercraft and a police helicopter. However, the confusion over how many people they were searching for and a lack of accurate information on the location of the cockle pickers hampered rescue attempts. Sue Todd, the coordinator of the coastguard centre in Crosby, Merseyside, who oversaw the operation, later said they were unsure if they were looking for as few as thirteen or as many as eighty people. More and more resources were sent to the area, with local fishermen, mountain rescue units and RAF helicopters all searching across Morecambe Bay. The rescue operation was one of the largest ever launched in North West England, but the incoming tide and bitterly cold conditions soon meant that there was little hope for anyone left out on the bay. Only a single survivor was found by one of the helicopters, stranded on a small raised outcrop of rocks in an area known as Priest Skear, desperately waving his hands in the air to attract the attention of the helicopter crew. An RNLI lifeboat was directed to him, and he became the only person the rescue operation could save, bringing the total number of survivors to fifteen. Twenty-one bodies would later be recovered from Morecambe Bay, but it was believed that there were two further cockle pickers with the group whose bodies have never been recovered or identified, raising the number of dead to twenty-three.

Investigations Begin

The following day, the disaster received high levels of coverage in the national news and was also picked up by many international media outlets. The treatment of illegal immigrants by gangmasters was thrust into the national debate, with many members of the public expressing their outrage that powerless immigrants who had come to the UK under the pretence of building a better life could end up effectively working as forced labourers with the vast majority of the public unaware of their plight. A major investigation, codenamed Operation Lund, was launched by Lancashire Police to establish exactly what had happened and to bring those responsible to account.

British police officers travelled to China to make inquiries and liaise with the families of the cockle pickers and begin the process of identifying the bodies of the dead. An officer of Chinese descent from Greater Manchester Police was also seconded to the investigation to act as an interpreter and use his knowledge of Chinese culture to assist with the investigation. The Home Office later worked to repatriate the bodies of the dead back to China.

Lin Liang Ren, Zhao Xiao Qing and Lin Mu Yong failed in their bid to pose as survivors, although they were aided by some of the genuine survivors who had been coerced to say that the gangmasters who organised the cockle picking died with the others on the bay. In an edition of *The Journal of Homicide and Major Incident Investigation*, which was published in 2006, Detective Superintendent Mick Gradwell, who worked on the investigation, gave an insight into the complexities of the case. He said that following their release the survivors:

> Were scared and reluctant to come forward and cooperate …
> They viewed the UK police with significant mistrust; this may
> have been because they had come to the country illegally,
> because of the language barrier or their lack of understanding
> of the British police and criminal justice system.

He went on to say that the survivors were looked after by the National Asylum Support Service, with many later moving away from the Morecambe area and into Chinese communities throughout the UK. When it came to finding them to become witnesses, it was found that many had given false or incomplete details, whereas others had little idea of their address. Some had simply put their name and '55 Liverpool' or 'Zone 2 London' as their contact details. Despite this, several survivors were successfully contacted, and after a long process of building trust with the Chinese community and assuring the survivors who came forward as witnesses that they would be protected, twelve survivors gave formal witness statements to the police.

Criminal Charges and Trial

Lin Liang Ren was charged with twenty-one counts of manslaughter, perverting the course of justice and immigration offences. His girlfriend, Zhao Xiao Qing, was also charged with three offences of perverting the course of justice and breaching immigration laws. Lin Mu Yong was charged with facilitation (assisting others to break immigration laws). The prosecution put forward the case that Lin Liang Ren rented the houses in Liverpool and Morecambe where immigrants who had been trafficked into Britain would stay and drove them to the locations where they would work as shellfish pickers. He would also arrange for the shellfish they gathered to be sold. Lin Liang Ren also made bogus applications for cockling permits, assisted by Zhao Xiao Qing. She helped to find properties to rent and acquire vehicles for the illegal cockling operations. Lin Mu Yong acted as Lin Liang Ren's second-in-command.

A British father and son, David Anthony Eden Snr and David Anthony Eden Jnr, who owned a local fish merchant business, were also charged with offences relating to helping the group break immigration law. It was alleged that the pair had agreed to buy the cockles, which would have been picked that night for a price substantially below the normal market value. In September 2005, the trial began at Preston Crown Court, with all of the defendants pleading not guilty to the charges against them. Due to the number of witnesses and the case's complexity, the trial was set to last between four and six months.

At the start of the trial, the jury and the judge, Mr Justice Henriques, were taken out across Morecambe Bay by hovercraft to Warton Sands, where the cockle picking took place. They then stayed out as the tide came in, allowing them to see the speed at which the bay filled with water and channels which had been small and easy to cross at low tide became deep and impassable as the tide cut the whole area off from the shore. The jury was also told that the calm conditions on that September day were very different to the cold, rainy and blustery February night when the cockle pickers lost their lives. The five defendants waived their right to accompany the judge and jurors on the visit.

The defence for Lin Liang Ren claimed that he was not in charge of the cockle pickers, meaning that he could not be responsible for their manslaughter. They stated that the deaths had been a tragic accident, and even if the cockle pickers had left Warton Sands at the correct time, they may have still lost their lives due to the exceptional weather conditions. The defence blamed the authorities for allowing cockle picking on Warton Sands, the police for not enforcing immigration law, and the Coast Guard for failing to monitor the area adequately.

Cedric Robinson, the Queen's Guide to the Sands at the time of the disaster, was called to the trial as an expert witness. Under questioning from the defence's legal team, he said that he found it difficult to believe that the North Wales and North West Sea Fisheries Committee had reopened the shellfish beds at Warton Sands and called the decision "madness" which had created "a disaster waiting to happen." He also said that his advice had not been sought before the reopening of the shellfish beds. Trevor Fleming was one of the local fishermen who had tried to warn the Chinese cockle pickers of the danger they were in. At the trial, he said that anyone going out onto the sands was putting their life at risk and that he believed a tragic accident would eventually happen.

The only person saved by the rescue operation, 26-year-old Li Hua, was called to give evidence. He explained that he could not stand the cold and rain, so he began to walk back to the shore when the cockle picking was only half complete, meaning he was already part of the way back to safety when the tide started to come in. Despite this, he tried to return to Warton Sands to assist the other cockle pickers when he realised how much danger they were in and was walking back to the group when the police helicopter located him. At the trial, the jury was shown video footage recorded from the helicopter of Li Hua waving and signalling for attention as the water rose around him. At the trial, he sobbed as he gave evidence from behind a screen and said:

> I never expected so many people to die, including Wen [the friend he was trying to rescue]. The water was up to my nose and mouth. I tried to swim, but the wave was quite big and I couldn't. ... I thought at the time I was going to die.

Li Hua had paid 190,000 yuan (£13,600) to gangmasters to be taken to Britain. The money had been given to him by his mother who had taken out a loan against her house to raise the sum. Recordings of the phone calls the cockle pickers made to relatives back in China were also played to the jury. One of the dead cockle pickers, Guo Bing Long, a married 28-year-old with two children, had called his wife in China and said:

> I am up to my chest in water. Maybe I am going to die. It's a tiny mistake by my boss. He mistook the time. He should have called us back an hour ago ... Tell the family to pray for me. It's too close. I am dying.

Verdicts

In March 2006, Lin Liang Ren and Zhao Xiao Qing were both found guilty of helping people break immigration law and perverting the course of justice. Lin Mu Yong was found guilty of facilitation. David Anthony

Eden Snr and David Anthony Eden Jnr were found not guilty. When they were sentenced, Mr Justice Henriques said that Lin Liang Ren was guilty of "cynically and callously" exploiting the workers and said that had he contacted the authorities at the first opportunity instead of waiting almost an hour, there may have been no loss of life. He was sentenced to fourteen years in jail. Zhao Xiao Qing was sentenced to two years and nine months, and Lin Mu Yong was sentenced to four years and ten months. While the Edens had been found not guilty, their application to have their costs paid was refused by the judge. The BBC reported that this was because they had lied to the police when questioned about the importance of cockling to their business.

After the trial, more information about Lin Liang Ren came to light, with the BBC running an article about him. The article describes Lin Liang Ren as looking "pasty-faced", "scruffy" and "every inch the crime victim" in pictures which were taken of him after the disaster as he tried to pose as one of the victims. The reality was that he was from an affluent family from Fuqing City in southeast China. He was highly educated and a qualified accountant who had previously worked as the head of finance in a Chinese plastics company that employed more than 900 people. He had arrived in Britain on a student visa in 2000, enrolling on various courses at unaccredited educational institutions in London and Manchester which exist only to provide illegitimate student visas to allow people to stay in the country illegally. In Britain, he soon became involved in trafficking Chinese workers to the country, lying to them about the type of work they would be doing and the amount of money they would earn. While Lin Liang Ren would send the workers he controlled to complete menial, unpleasant and sometimes dangerous tasks, he would never participate in the work himself. On the day of the disaster, he had been waiting in his van while his workers lost their lives on the beach. The BBC reported that he told police "I don't like the cold and I don't like the water." According to the *Independent*, Lin Liang Ren lived a lavish lifestyle. Fish merchants would meet him at the shoreline with thousands of pounds in cash to buy the cockles and other shellfish gathered by the groups he controlled.

Lin Liang Ren was known to frequent casinos in Liverpool where he would gamble up to £600 per hand on blackjack tables and was often seen driving around the city in his Mitsubishi sports car.

In 2014, news emerged that Lin Liang Ren had been released from prison after serving half his sentence. He had served another two years on licence and was then deported back to China. The news was met with outrage from the victims' families, who pointed out that Lin Liang Ren had only served four months in jail for each life lost. David Morris, the Conservative Member of Parliament for Morecambe and Lunesdale, spoke out against the decision to release Lin Liang Ren. He submitted an early day motion in parliament that asked about the status of Lin Liang Ren, Zhao Xiao Qing, and Lin Mu Yong. Part of the motion read:

> The people of Morecambe deserve to know how many years each served in prison in the UK and ... when they were deported and whether they are currently incarcerated in their native China.

While the Ministry of Justice initially said that it did not comment on individual cases, it later emerged that it was not known if Lin Liang Ren was jailed or allowed to go free when he arrived back in China. It was also revealed that Zhao Xiao Qing was released after one year in jail and deported to China in 2007, and Lin Mu Yong was deported in 2008.

Reform of Cockling in Morecambe Bay

Despite the deaths of the cockle pickers, it took a long time to reform the laws and legislation governing cockle picking in Morecambe Bay. An article in the *Guardian* outlined that in 2009 the cockle beds were still a "free for all" with an estimated 800 to 900 people coming to Morecambe from all over the country to pick cockles each year. This eventually ended when a new system of Inshore Fisheries and Conservation Authorities (IFCAs) was established in 2011 and became responsible for the cockle beds. The North Western IFCA implemented a highly regulated permit system for cockle pickers. This ensured that everyone who ventured out onto the sands of Morecambe Bay and the surrounding areas was properly trained and experienced in shellfish collecting. Since the permit system has been introduced there has been a drastic reduction in the number of times search and rescue teams have had to be called out to rescue cockle pickers from Morecambe Bay. As of 2023, only around 150 permits for cockle picking were issued, and the North Western IFCA can close the cockle beds if they are likely become dangerous due to weather or sea conditions.

Memorials

A memorial plaque showing the names of the cockle pickers who lost their lives and a poem, *The Bay of Words*, was erected near Morecambe Promenade in 2007. By 2020 the plaque had fallen into disrepair and was replaced. The new plaque showed the same poem and names, but this time featured an engraving of a red-crowned crane, the national bird of China. A limestone sculpture of a man praying in a kneeling position was unveiled in Bolton-le-Sands in 2013. The sculpture named *Praying Shell* was created by Anthony Padgett. Although plans for this sculpture pre-date the cockle picking disaster, it has also become seen as a memorial, as it overlooks the area where the cockle pickers lost their lives.

In February 2024 a service was conducted on the shoreline at Morecambe close to where the cockle pickers lost their lives to commemorate the twentieth anniversary of the disaster. Over one hundred people attended, including members of local Chinese community associations. Lanterns were lit and lines from a poem about the tragedy by the writer Lemn Sissay were chalked onto a sea wall.

Chapter 7

FV *Antares*

The FV *Antares* was a small trawler which fished in the waters of the Firth of Clyde off the west coast of Scotland. In the early hours of 22 November 1990, the *Antares* sank, with all four crewmembers losing their lives. The Royal Navy submarine HMS *Trenchant* would later be found to be responsible for the loss of the *Antares*, leading to anger across the fishing communities of western Scotland, and major changes in the way Royal Navy submarines operated.

The Firth of Clyde is the semi-enclosed mouth of the River Clyde on the west coast of Scotland. It is around 40 kilometres (25 miles) across and features some of the deepest waters anywhere around the coastline of Britain. While fish stocks have declined around the Firth of Clyde in recent decades, it is still home to numerous commercial fishing vessels. A large Royal Navy base was constructed at Gare Loch, an open sea loch at the Firth of Clyde, during the Second World War. Since the 1960s it has been home to the UK's fleet of nuclear and conventionally armed submarines.

The *Antares*

The *Antares* was built in Sandhaven, Aberdeenshire, in 1965 and operated out of Carradale. The 34-ton vessel was 17 metres (53 ft) long and was mainly constructed out of wood. It was capable of a speed of 8 knots

(9 mph) and was equipped with a six-man inflatable life raft and other safety features such as distress rockets and lifebuoys. It had a crew of four and was owned and skippered by 33-year-old Jamie Russell.

The *Antares* would typically leave Carradale on the east side of Kintyre late on a Sunday night to fish in the Firth of Clyde, staying out at sea until Thursday night, although periodic visits to port would be made to unload catches. On 18 November 1990, the crew set out as usual to fish the deep waters of Bute Sound, which separates the Isle of Arran from the Isle of Bute. The *Antares* made the one-hour journey to the town of Largs on 20 November and again the following day to unload catches before returning to Bute Sound. Jamie Russell maintained radio communication with the skippers of two other trawlers, *Heroine* and *Hercules III*, which were fishing in the same area. Typically, the *Antares* trawled along the trench of Bute Sound for four hours, then made a 180-degree turn, and trawled back along the trench for another four hours before turning around again and repeating the process. This is how the vessel was operating in the early hours of 22 November, in calm sea conditions with excellent visibility. At approximately 2.00 am, the watchkeeper of the *Heroine* spotted the *Antares* engaged in normal fishing. This would be the last ever sighting of the vessel.

HMS *Trenchant* and the Perisher Course

Four days earlier, on 17 November, HMS *Trenchant*, an 85-metre (280 ft) long, 5,3000-ton nuclear-powered submarine of the Royal Navy, entered the Firth of Clyde. *Trenchant* had been at sea since 12 November and was engaged in a training course for officers seeking to become submarine commanders. Officially called the Submarine Command Course, but almost always referred to as the Perisher, the 24-week course is regarded as one of the most challenging command courses carried out by any navy in the world and must be passed for an officer to take command of their own submarine. There are multiple stages to the Perisher; if a candidate fails any stage, they are immediately removed from the submarine by helicopter or boat and cannot serve in any part of the submarine service for the rest of their Royal Navy career.

When the Perisher course was being carried out, the submarine's commander would pass control of the vessel to another senior officer who was acting as the course commander. He would, in turn, allow one of the officer candidates (referred to as 'students' in the Perisher terminology) to take control of the vessel while he observed and assessed their performance. The *Trenchant* was in the Firth of Clyde to carry out an exercise with HMS *Charybdis*, a Leander-class frigate. Four student officers had started the Perisher course on board HMS *Trenchant*, but two had already been removed from the submarine due to failing one of the preceding stages.

A mock minelaying exercise was carried out which went on until the early hours of 22 November. The student officer who had command of the submarine was required to lay mines while avoiding detection by HMS *Charybdis*. Once this was completed, the submarine had to ascend to periscope depth and launch a simulated attack on the frigate. Just after 2.00 am, having completed the mine laying exercise and simulated attack, HMS *Trenchant* submerged to a depth of 60 metres (196 ft) and maintained a steady course. At this time, the *Trenchant*'s commander was in the wardroom discussing the student's performance with the course leader while the duty commander was preparing to restart the Perisher course with the other student in command of the submarine.

The Collision

While at periscope depth for the simulated attack, HMS *Charybdis* had been the only vessel on the surface, but three new surface contacts had then appeared on *Trenchant*'s sonar. One was a small cargo ship which was growing fainter as it moved away from HMS *Trenchant*, but the two other new contacts, both identified as fishing boats, were getting closer. The crew in the forward sonar room communicated the situation regarding surface contacts to the control room through the submarine's speaker system. They reported that one of the fishing boats, designated as 'Contact 05', was growing louder and approaching the submarine from starboard. The duty commander, therefore, ordered the *Trenchant* to move to port. The fishing boat passed within 180 metres (200 yds) of *Trenchant*, but less than a minute later, loud banging noises were heard coming from the starboard side of the submarine, followed by the sound of something scraping along the submarine's hull.

Unsure of what had just happened, the *Trenchant* returned to periscope depth, although this took around ten minutes as it had to move to a new position to ensure they were clear of surface vessels. During the ascent, a crew member operating underwater listening equipment reported hearing a "disturbance of the sea", although little significance was placed on this at the time. At the surface, control of the submarine was handed back to the commander, and a visual check of the area was made, with two fishing boats – *Heroine* and *Hercules III* – being sighted. The crew then inspected the submarine and found a trawl warp wire wrapped around the submarine's sonar dome, and it became apparent that they had collided with a fishing boat's trawl gear. As there were two close surface contacts detected while submerged, and two fishing boats visible and fishing normally on the surface, the crew of the *Trenchant* believed that the collision had been a relatively minor incident, with no serious damage caused to the fishing boat it had come into contact with.

Radio contact was made with HMS *Charybdis*, and it was established that neither of the fishing boats had tried to contact the frigate. *Charybdis* reported that nothing unusual had been sighted, and there was nothing of significance to report. The trawl warp wire was removed from the sonar dome using bolt cutters. HMS *Charybdis* was again radioed and repeated that no fishing boats had contacted them to report being in distress. The *Trenchant*'s commander tried radioing the *Heroine* and *Hercules III* but could not make contact. Seeing that both fishing boats still appeared to be engaged in normal fishing and HMS *Charybdis* had nothing to report, the commander of HMS *Trenchant* contacted Faslane. He explained that they had collided with a trawler's nets, but the trawler appeared to be safe and had continued fishing. HMS *Trenchant* then submerged and restarted the Perisher exercise with a new student officer in command of the submarine.

But the crew and commander of HMS *Trenchant* had made a momentous error in their analysis of the situation. Contact 05 had not been a single vessel but had been both the *Antares* and *Heroine*, which were in close proximity as they passed each other. There should have been three trawlers operating on the surface, not two. HMS *Trenchant* had collided with the *Antares*'s warp wires (the cables connecting the nets to the fishing vessel), pulling the fishing boat violently to starboard and then causing it to capsize. As the submarine continued forward, the *Antares* was pulled under the water in an inverted position – this was the cause of the banging and scraping sounds heard on board the *Trenchant*. Eventually, the warp wires snapped, releasing the *Antares*, which floated back to the surface, keel upwards. It is unknown how long the *Antares* would have remained in this position, but as the wheelhouse window was open to allow the skipper to observe the turn manoeuvre he was conducting, water ingress would have been rapid, and the *Antares* may have only remained on the surface for minutes. The disturbance of the sea the crew of the *Trenchant* heard (and disregarded as unimportant) was the sound of the *Antares* sinking to the seabed. With the command team of the *Trenchant* informing Faslane that all fishing boats were accounted for, no one was aware that *Antares* was missing. It would be almost ten hours before a full-scale search and rescue operation was launched.

The Rescue Operation Belatedly Begins

Following HMS *Trenchant*'s message to Faslane, staff at Faslane informed Clyde Marine Rescue Coordination Centre (MRCC) that there had been an incident between a submarine and a trawler, and a radio message was sent out to all fishing boats in the area. The secretary of the Clyde Fishermen's

Association was also informed of the incident. He was immediately concerned, being fully aware that the small, wooden trawlers which fished the Firth of Clyde would not simply continue fishing normally after a nuclear submarine collided with their nets. On the morning of 22 November, he contacted the Clyde MRCC and told them that action needed to be taken to ensure that all of the fishing boats which were out the previous night were safe. He then began telephoning staff at the early morning fish auctions to see if any fishing boat had failed to arrive with its catch.

It was almost 10.00 am when MRCC began contacting individual fishing boats and informing the skippers that there may have been a serious incident in the early hours of that morning. After speaking to the skipper of *Heroine*, the staff at Clyde MRCC realised that it must have been the *Antares* that was involved in the incident. Attempts were made to contact the *Antares* via the vessel's cellnet telephone, but no contact could be made. A search of ports and harbours was made to see if the *Antares* had returned to shore, but no trace of the vessel could be found. A helicopter was scrambled from the Royal Navy Air Station at Prestwick to search the area where HMS *Trenchant* reported colliding with the trawl nets. Fish boxes and oil were sighted on the water's surface, and, at last, a full-scale search and rescue operation was launched.

At midday, HMS *Trenchant* returned to Faslane. An inspection revealed that the damage caused by the trawl net was more severe than initially realised, as the crew could not see the full extent of the damage while the submarine was at sea. In the official report into the incident, this was listed as the starboard log probe being sheared off, a pinger and the bolts which held it in place being ripped away and its base plate badly bent, the leading edges of the starboard fin being badly damaged and further minor damage to the starboard side of the submarine.

By the early afternoon, the search for the *Antares* was in full effect. *Heroine* and *Hercules III* had stopped fishing and began searching for the *Antares* and were joined by other fishing boats that had also broken off from fishing and made their way to the area. HMS *Charybdis* also returned to coordinate the search, and many volunteers began to look for the *Antares* from the shore. A sonar search of the area where the *Antares* was last seen was carried out by *Heroine* and *Hercules III*, and a new wreck was discovered on the seabed. While this was believed to be the *Antares*, the search continued, as the crew could have escaped the vessel in their life raft. The search continued with around forty ships, most of which were fishing boats, but, at 4.30 pm, with darkness setting in, the search was called off. It was accepted that with the number of vessels searching, the *Antares* or its life raft would have been found if they were on the surface, and the water temperature and weather conditions meant that if the crew had been in the water with only the wreckage of the boat to cling onto they would not have survived. In the early hours of the following day, a Royal Fleet Auxiliary vessel confirmed that the new wreck was that of the *Antares*. Searches for the bodies of the crew or any wreckage from the *Antares* continued at sea and across shorelines for the next few days, but nothing was found.

MAIB Investigation and Report

Several Royal Fleet Auxiliary ships and diving support vessels were sent to the area where the *Antares* was located, and divers were used to investigate the wreck, managing to recover the bodies of three of the four crewmembers. Work was then started to make the wreck of the *Antares* safe for recovery. On 9 December, the vessel RMAS *Wilchief* lifted the wreck to shallow water in Kilchattan Bay on the Isle of Bute, where an initial analysis was made. Although water pressure and immersion in seawater had damaged many of the controls and equipment, it could be ascertained that *Antares*'s engine was set to full ahead, the VHF radio was switched on, and the life raft had failed to detach. The body of the fourth crewmember could not be located but would eventually be recovered in a net by a trawler in April of the following year.

The wreck was raised to the surface and towed to a harbour in Greenock, arriving on 11 December. After a more detailed analysis, it was found that snapped trawl wires on the *Antares* matched those wrapped around the sonar dome of HMS *Trenchant*, confirming that the submarine had caused the *Antares* to sink. It was also found that the life raft, which should have automatically detached when the *Antares* sank, had been improperly stored which prevented this from happening.

The Marine Accident Investigation Branch (MAIB), the UK government agency responsible for investigating all maritime accidents in British waters, began their analysis of the wreck. A comprehensive further investigation was carried out, the findings of which were compiled into an official report published in 1992. The report stated that after the Perisher course was completed, there was a lowering of alertness among the submarine's crew, the command team having a "false sense of security" that they were clear of surface contacts. The report stated that between the end of the Perisher course and the collision with the *Antares*'s nets, the crew of the *Trenchant* never had an accurate picture of surface contacts. However, the most serious error was the belief that Contact 05 was a single vessel when it was two fishing boats passing each other. The confusion caused by the command of the submarine passing between different duty commanders and students taking the Perisher course was listed as another contributory factor. Furthermore, the report stated that the command team of the *Trenchant* should have known that snagging the nets of a trawler to such an extent that trawl warps were embedded into the submarine's sonar dome was a serious incident and it would have been impossible for a trawler to continue fishing normally after this had happened. The report went on to say that the crew of HMS *Trenchant* had "a lack of appreciation of the reality of the situation."

Another major failure regarded the 'disturbance of the sea' that a crewmember reported hearing, which was almost certainly the sound of the Antares sinking to the seabed. This was clear evidence that a serious incident with a surface vessel had occurred, but it appears to have been disregarded by the crewmember who heard it, and it is not known if the command team of the *Trenchant* were even made aware. Once on the surface, the *Trenchant*'s attempts to take stock of the situation and ensure that all surface vessels were safe and accounted for were also criticised. While *Trenchant* did contact HMS *Charybdis* and informed Faslane of what had happened, this was deemed insufficient. As radio contact with *Heroine* and *Hercules III* could not be established, the crew of *Trenchant* should have used signal lamps to communicate with the fishing vessels. Had contact been made, they may have learned that the *Antares* should also have been present and that they had caused its sinking.

The main findings of the report were that a "partial breakdown in both the structure and the standards of watchkeeping on board *Trenchant*" was the main reason for the sinking of the *Antares* and the four crewmembers losing their lives. It was also stated that the *Antares* was engaged in normal fishing and there was no way the crew could have known about the presence of the *Trenchant* beneath them, meaning: "no blame can, therefore, be attached to *Antares*." However, it was pointed out that the deficient storage position of the life raft prevented it from floating free, and this may have been a contributing factor to the loss of life.

Recommendations and Court-Martial

The report made several recommendations which the Royal Navy would have to implement. The minimum distance that submerged submarines should maintain from surface vessels was increased from 1,830 metres (2,000 yds) to 2,740 metres (3,000 yds). This distance should, if possible, be increased to 3,660 metres (4,000 yds) if fishing vessels are encountered to ensure that the submarine stays clear of towed fishing gear. Submarines should also travel on the surface unless they are actively engaged in exercises, and Admiralty charts should be updated to show the areas where submarines are most likely to be active. Plans were also made for Royal Navy submarines to be equipped with listening technology which could identify the fish-finding echo sounders used by trawlers to allow submarines to pinpoint the location of fishing vessels, but the Royal Navy said that this was too complicated to implement as fish finding equipment used too wide an array of frequencies.

Finally, the Ministry of Defence was made to undertake a full review of its fishing vessel avoidance protocols and ensure that the lessons which had been learned following the loss of the *Antares* were disseminated to all submarine crews. No recommendations were made to alter or change the Perisher course in any way. There were also several recommendations for commercial fishermen. The importance of constantly monitoring the VHF radio was stressed. Further recommendations were made on the correct storage of life rafts to ensure they were deployed properly when a fishing vessel began to sink.

In June 1992, Lieutenant Commander Peter McDonnell, who had been in command of the *Trenchant* while undertaking the Perisher course when the submarine collided with the *Antares*'s nets, was court-martialled. He was found guilty and severely reprimanded by the Royal Navy. However, it soon became apparent that no further action would be taken against the more senior officers on board the *Trenchant* at the time of the incident. This caused anger amongst both the family of the *Antares*'s crew and the wider community. George Foulkes, the Labour MP for Carrick, Cumnock and Doon Valley, campaigned for further action against the *Trenchant*'s senior officers and stronger restrictions on submarine activity in fishing areas. The *Herald* newspaper quoted him as saying:

> It is clear that a junior officer under training, Lieutenant Commander Peter McDonnell, has been made the scapegoat in this instance ... Without any deterrent action by the commander-in-chief and with no ban on submerged activity in fishing areas, the seas where submarines operate remain a constant danger for fishermen.

Despite this, Archibald Hamilton, Minister of State for the Armed Forces, announced in October 1992 that no other crewmembers would be court-martialled, nor would any other disciplinary action be taken against the crew of the *Trenchant*, effectively closing the matter. The government also announced it had been decided that the measures put in place to prevent a repeat of the incident were sufficient, and submarine exercises would continue in the Firth of Forth and the surrounding areas under the new regulations.

The Wreck of the *Antares*, Memorials and Similar Incidents

The wreck of the *Antares* was restored and moved to the Scottish Maritime Museum in Irvine, North Ayrshire. In 2008, the increasing cost of maintaining the vessel meant the decision was made for the *Antares* to be dismantled and scrapped. The four crewmembers of the *Antares* – Jamie Russell, Billy Martindale, Dugald John Campbell and Stewart Campbell are memorialised on a plaque at Carradale Harbour.

In 2016, it emerged that there had been a fishing boat and submarine collision incident the previous year in the waters of the Irish Sea. The *Karen* was trawling for prawns out of Ardglass, one of Northern Ireland's busiest fishing ports, when it was dragged backwards for around fifteen miles with its stern submerged until the trawl warps eventually snapped, freeing the vessel. Although the deck of the *Karen* was damaged and parts of the boat had been ripped away, the crew were unharmed. The Royal Navy were unaware that the incident had occurred until hours later. The MAIB later carried out an inquiry into the incident and found that the crew of the submarine, which has not been identified, believed that they were passing underneath a cargo vessel as they could not detect the noise trawl nets made, and therefore thought they had left sufficient space to avoid a collision.

Steve Clinch, the chief inspector of marine accidents at the MAIB, said:

> The accident happened because of insufficient passage planning by the submarine's command team and their failure to follow guidance on fishing vessel avoidance. Had its trawl

warps not parted, it is almost inevitable that *Karen* would have capsized and sunk.

The report went on to say that the submarine's crew had failed to follow the procedures which were introduced after the sinking of the *Antares*, with Clinch adding: "The reluctance of the Royal Navy to fully engage in the subsequent investigation resulted in this report taking significantly longer to deliver than would normally be the case ... By its actions, the Royal Navy also needs to rebuild trust with the fishing industry."

When news of the incident with the *Karen* broke, it raised fears that the lessons learned through the loss of the *Antares* were being forgotten and that another similar incident could happen again. The Royal Navy is believed to have paid compensation to the crew and owner of the *Karen*, with a spokesperson telling the *Telegraph* that they had "revised our procedures to reduce the risk that such an incident could happen again" and said that they "continue to work closely with the maritime community to maximise safety."

Chapter 8

Solway Harvester

The *Solway Harvester* was a Scottish fishing boat that sank in the Irish Sea in the year 2000. The crew of seven all lost their lives. While the loss of the vessel was initially a mystery, it soon emerged that there were multiple safety issues with the *Solway Harvester*, leading to legal action against the vessel's owner and new guidelines and regulations being put in place for British fishing boats.

The *Solway Harvester* was a dredger registered to the port of Ballantrae in South Ayrshire, Scotland but often operated out of Kirkcudbright on the north coast of the Solway Firth. Its main areas of operation were in the Irish Sea, around the Isle of Man and the north coast of Wales. Businessman Richard Gidney owned the *Solway Harvester* and was its first skipper, but he stood down in 1995 to concentrate on running his business, RG Holdings Limited. Through this company, he owned and operated several other fishing boats, as well as Deeside Marine Limited, a Kirkcudbright-based marine engineering company which carried out repairs and maintenance of the vessels Gidney owned.

As a dredger – a fishing vessel which gathered shellfish by dragging heavy metal cages, known as dredges, across the seabed – the *Solway Harvester* mainly targeted large king scallops and a smaller species of scallops known as queenies. It was a relatively large fishing vessel, being 19.5 metres (64 ft) long and had a lightship weight (the weight of the ship with no crew, cargo or fuel on board) of 166 tons. It operated with a crew of seven – the captain, mate and five deckhands.

FV *Gaul*

A memorial to the *Gaul* in Hull.

One of the memorial boards in Hull, showing the lives of fishermen lost over the years, including those on board the *Gaul*.

The derelict Lord Line Building in Hull where the *Gaul* once docked. Once the centre of the city's fishing industry, it has been abandoned for many decades.

The Eyemouth Fishing Disaster

Eyemouth Disaster Memorial. (Kim Traynor, Wikimedia Commons)

Entrance to Eyemouth Harbour. (Adam D. Hop, Wikimedia Commons)

Ehime Maru and USS Greeneville Collision

USS *Greeneville* in Dry Dock #1 at the Pearl Harbor Naval Shipyard Maintenance Facility on 21 February 2001 following the collision with the *Ehime Maru.* (Public domain image as the work of a U.S. military or Department of Defense employee, taken or made as part of that person's official duties, Wikimedia Commons)

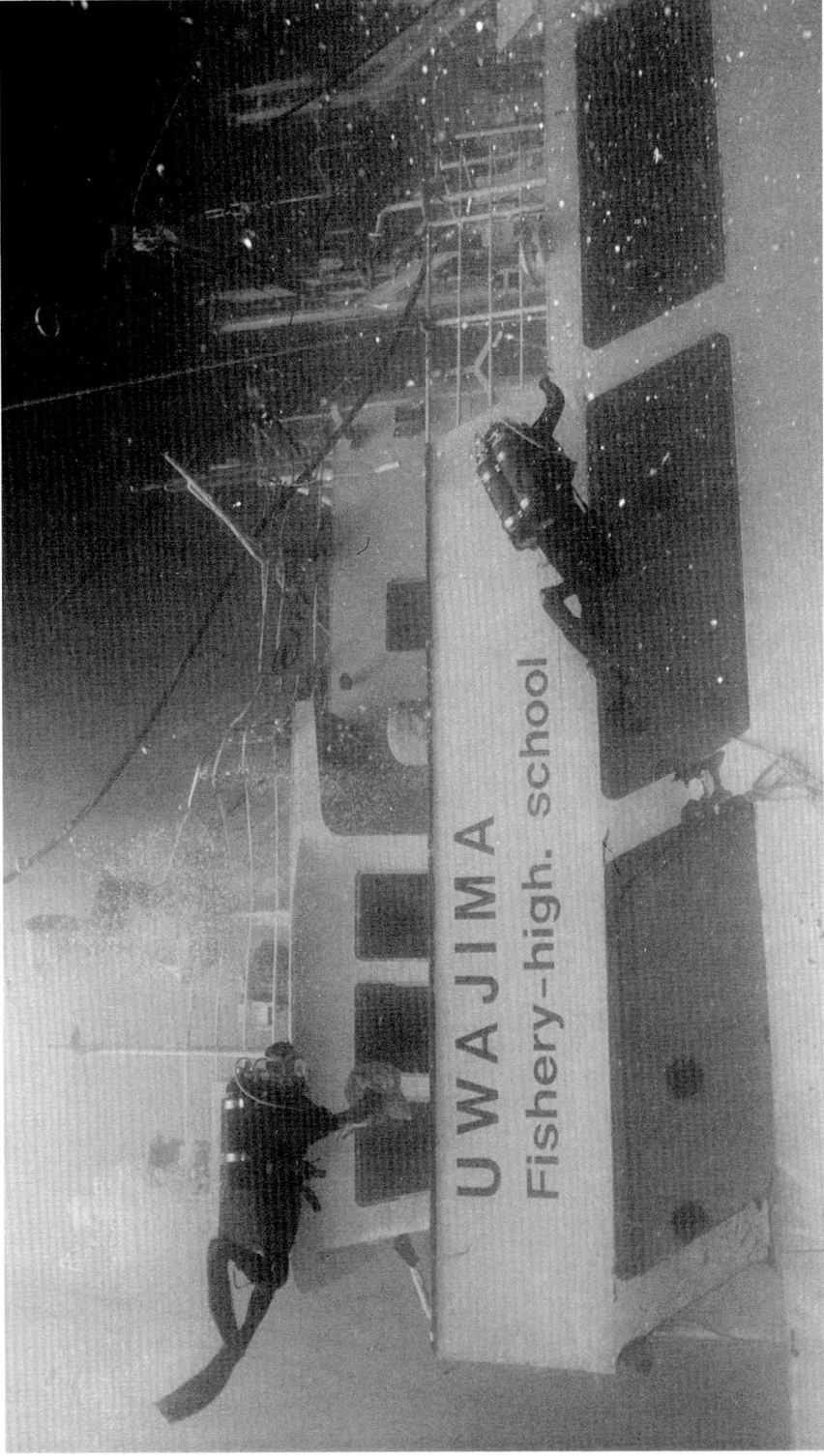

Recovery of the *Ehime Maru*. (Public domain image as the work of a U.S. military or Department of Defense employee, taken or made as part of that person's official duties, Wikimedia Commons)

Ehime Maru memorial at Kakaako Waterfront Park in Honolulu Hawaii. (Public domain image as the work of a U.S. military or Department of Defense employee, taken or made as part of that person's official duties, Wikimedia Commons)

The *Bugaled Breizh*

The wreck of the *Bugaled Brezih* preserved at Brest Arsenal following the disaster. (Anthonydela, Wikimedia Commons)

The Morecambe Bay Cockling Disaster

Morecambe Bay: (The Air Base, Wikimedia Commons)

The Loss of FV *Antares*

HMS *Trenchant* pictured in 2017. (Public domain image as the work of a U.S. military or Department of Defense employee, taken or made as part of that person's official duties, Wikimedia Commons)

Solway Harvester

The wreck of the *Solway Harvester* at Douglas, Isle of Man. (Richard Hoare / Wreck of the ''Solway Harvester'' Douglas / CC BY-SA 2.0, Geograph.org.uk)

Solway Harvester Memorial. (David Dixon, Geograph.org.uk)

The 1914 Newfoundland Sealing Disasters

SS *Newfoundland* with Captain Westbury Kean [inset], taken from Newfoundland Quarterly Summer 1914. (Image copyright-free due to age of image, Wikimedia Commons)

Crew of the *Bellaventure* bringing *Newfoundland* survivors onto their ship. (Image copyright-free due to age of image, Wikimedia Commons)

The *Stephano* pictured in 1911. (Image copyright-free due to age of image, Wikimedia Commons)

The Seaham Lifeboat Disaster

The restored *George Elmy* lifeboat, pictured in Seaham in May 2024. (Self-taken photograph)

The memorial to the Seaham Lifeboat Disaster. (Self-taken photograph)

Seaham Harbour pictured in 2011. (Steve Daniels, Geograph.org.uk)

Richard Gidney appointed Andrew Mills (known as Craig) as the skipper of the *Solway Harvester* in 1997. Mills was successful in this role, with the year ending 1999 being the vessel's most profitable ever, with the *Solway Harvester* generating over £500,000 for Gidney's company. Mills had a high level of responsibility in running the *Solway Harvester*. He hired and fired crewmembers, arranged maintenance, refuelling and repairs of the vessel, organised food and other provisions for fishing expeditions and was ultimately accountable for the safety of the crew when at sea.

Vessel Defects and the Flooding of the Fish Room

In 1995, three months after Gidney left his role as the *Solway Harvester*'s skipper (but before Mills was appointed), the Maritime Safety Agency (MSA) inspected the vessel. Numerous defects and shortcomings were discovered, many of which related to essential safety equipment. Fire extinguishers, line throwers (devices to cast lines and ropes long distances) and parachute flares all needed to be provided for the vessel. Furthermore, the hydrostatic release unit for the emergency position-indicating radiobeacon needed renewing, smoke/light makers used to show if a ship was in distress were required, as was a medical chest, and the engine room door seal needed repairing. The following year, the *Solway Harvester* was again inspected during the process of renewing its UK Fishing vessel certificate. It was found that the *Solway Harvester* no longer met stability requirements. Gidney's company Deeside Marine was tasked with fitting new watertight bulkheads and informed the MSA by letter that the work had been completed. A new certificate was issued, which would remain valid until October 2000.

In 1997, shortly after Craig Mills had taken over as skipper, it became apparent that the fish room (the part of the ship where scallops were bagged and stored) was liable to flooding. This was because one of the watertight covers from the ice scuttle hatches – openings which allowed meat from scallops which had their shells removed on deck to be passed down to the fish room – was lost overboard and not replaced. Large amounts of excess water which splashed over the deck in rough weather could now downflood into the fish room via the opening. The Fishing Vessel (Safety Provisions) Regulations 1975, which the *Solway Harvester* was compelled to operate under, was clear that covers for the ice scuttle hatches were "essential for fishing operations" and must be "capable of being closed watertight."

Indeed, flooding of the fish room appeared to be an ongoing issue for the *Solway Harvester*. In late December 1999, the *Solway Harvester* set off from Kirkcudbright to fish in the Irish Sea. While the trip was successful in terms of catches, there had been an incident where the fish room had again flooded due to water ingress. The bilge pump, which should have pumped out the water to prevent this, had not functioned properly, leading to significant flooding of the fish room. The mate and deckhands had to use buckets to remove the water, and, as the vessel rolled from side to side in the heavy seas, a deckhand was knocked off his feet by the water sloshing from across the fish room, and several bags of scallops, which weighed around 50 kg (110 lbs) each, were thrown around and burst open. The floodwater appeared to have drained from the main deck into the fish room mostly through the open ice scuttle hatch, but other gaps allowed water to seep through, and the melting ice that catches were packed in had also caused a small amount of additional water to build up.

It appeared that the skipper and crew of the *Solway Harvester* were not particularly concerned about the flooding of the fish room or the missing ice scuttle hatch cover. They believed that only small amounts of water got into the fish room via the hatch, and the vessel's system of pumps could usually remove any water which did build up. Furthermore, if excess water did amass in the fish room the crew could bail it out using buckets before it became a problem. During the flooding incident in December 1999, dredging continued as normal, with three hauls of scallops being made as two crewmembers cleared the water out of the fish room. When the *Solway*

Harvester returned to harbour, there was no evidence that information on the flooding was passed on to the skippers of the other vessels operated by Gidney's company, or any official record of the incident being made.

The Crew and the Final Voyage

Just weeks later, in the first few days of January 2000, the crew of the *Solway Harvester* prepared for what would be its final voyage. But before they even set off there were multiple issues with the vessel. The pumps used to empty the fish room of water were not functioning correctly, and the bilge alarm which alerted the skipper if the fish room was beginning to fill with water was broken. Furthermore, the mate (second in command) of the *Solway Harvester* would miss the trip due to illness. No replacement could be found, so for the first stint at sea, there would be only be the skipper Craig Mills and five deckhands on board – meaning they would be operating with a crew of six instead of seven and have no mate on board. On 6 January the *Solway Harvester* left Kirkcudbright for its fishing grounds in the Irish Sea. Fishing was successful, with over two hundred bags of queenies and sixteen bags of king scallops being gathered. But there were further problems with the vessel's generator and engines. With no mate on board, the skipper had to stop the vessel and leave the wheelhouse to deal with these issues himself, as none of the crew had the required knowledge or expertise. On 9 January, the *Solway Harvester* docked at Whithorn and unloaded its catch. It also took on another crewmember to bring its complement back up to seven, although this was another deckhand and not a replacement for the missing mate.

Craig Mills was an experienced commercial fisherman. He had been going to sea since 1994 and became the skipper of the *Solway Harvester* in February 1997. He held a Class 2 Fishing Certificate of Competency and had previously skippered another vessel owned by Gidney's company. The rest of the crew for the final voyage consisted of his brother, 33-year-old Robin Mills. He was a painter and decorator who worked with his brother on the *Solway Harvester* when they required additional crewmembers. They were joined by 18-year-old David Mills (the cousin of Craig Mills), 22-year-old John Murphy and 26-year-old Martin Milligan. All had around two years of experience working on commercial fishing boats. Two 17-year-olds, Wesley Jolly and David Lyons, who had just months of fishing experience between them, were also on board. While this gave the *Solway Harvester* its full crew of seven, it meant that there was still no one to fulfil the role of mate, meaning the trip would effectively take place with a skipper and six deckhands, several of whom were very young with very little experience. Furthermore, Robin Mills, David Mills, Martin Milligan, and Wesley Jolly had not completed the basic safety training that was mandatory for anyone working on a commercial fishing boat.

For the second part of the trip, the *Solway Harvester* again sailed to the Irish Sea and began dredging, successfully filling more than 150 bags with scallops and queenies by the morning of 11 January. The *Solway Harvester*'s sister ship, the *Tobrach-N*, sailed to the same area, and the two dredgers fished within a few miles of each other. The weather was initially calm but began to worsen as the day progressed. Craig Mills was in constant radio contact with the skipper of the *Tobrach-N*, discussing both their catches and the changing weather conditions. In the mid-afternoon, with conditions continuing to deteriorate, both vessels hauled their dredges on board and made their way toward land, with Mills stating that he was heading to Ramsay Bay on the northeast coast of the Isle of Man. There, they would be able to shelter until conditions improved, and with no fishing taking place the crew would have time to eat a meal and rest. As the *Solway Harvester* made its way toward the Isle of Man, Mills made multiple phone calls. He contacted the company that bought the *Solway Harvester*'s catch, made arrangements with Deeside Marine to carry out repairs on the vessel and have the *Solway Harvester* refuelled when it returned to port. He also telephoned the crewmember who was missing the trip due to illness and had a conversation with his partner, who was at home. Although he said that the weather was "really wild" and "screaming" and that the *Solway Harvester* was "battened down", he did not say that there was anything amiss and gave the impression that they were dealing with the conditions well.

Mills continued to make calls. He spoke to the skipper of another of Gidney's boats, the *Kingfisher,* and telephoned the skipper of another fishing vessel, the *Q-Varl*, who was at home as his ship was undergoing repairs. In both of these calls, Mills did not say there were any problems and even remarked that the *Solway Harvester* was making steady progress despite the conditions.

Lost Contact and the Search for Survivors

At 5.47 pm, an emergency positioning radio beacon registered to the *Solway Harvester* sent a signal via satellite to Liverpool Maritime Rescue Subcentre indicating that the vessel was in distress. Richard Gidney, the *Solway Harvester*'s owner, was contacted and confirmed that the vessel was in the area indicated by the emergency beacon. After attempts to contact the *Solway Harvester* were unsuccessful, a full-scale search was initiated. Lifeboats and a helicopter were deployed from the Isle of Man, and the *Solway Harvester*'s sister ship, *Tobrach-N,* stopped fishing to join the search. Other nearby vessels, such as the Royal Fleet Auxiliary tanker RFA *Bayleaf* and the survey vessel *Humber Surveyor*, also diverted from their operations to search for the Solway Harvester.

Searching continued overnight, and the emergency positioning radio beacon was recovered from the sea. Analysis confirmed that it belonged to the *Solway Harvester* and had activated automatically. An unopened life raft canister from the *Solway Harvester* was also recovered from the sea, but there was no sign of the dredger itself or any survivors. Weather conditions continued to worsen with very rough seas, storm-force winds and heavy rain severely reducing visibility. Despite this, the search continued and the second life raft canister, also unopened, was recovered. At midday on 12 January, the *Humber Surveyor* conducted a sonar search of the seabed, and the wreck of the *Solway Harvester* was located eleven miles off the southeast coast of the Isle of Man, 35 metres (115 ft) below the surface. That evening, it was concluded that there was no hope of finding any survivors, and the search was called off.

Initial Investigations and Partial Recovery

The Marine Accident Investigation Branch (MAIB) immediately began its investigation into the loss of the *Solway Harvester*. A Royal Navy minehunter, HMS *Sandown*, was sent to the area and deployed a ROV (Remotely Operated Vehicle) to the wreck to carry out an initial assessment. This was soon followed by a much more detailed survey by the specialist vessel *Mansal 18* on 18 January. ROVs were again used to examine the wreck and search for bodies. Only the port side could be seen as the *Solway Harvester* was lying on its starboard side, but it could be ascertained that there was no significant damage to the hull, and the body of one crewmember was visible. In late January, a diving support vessel, CSO *Well Servicer*, set off from Barrow-in-Furness and headed to the wreck. On board were MAIB investigators, representatives of the *Solway Harvester's* owner and insurers and, as the sinking happened within the territorial waters of the Isle of Man, officers from the Isle of Man Constabulary.

On 30 January, divers were lowered to the wreck. They removed bags of scallops and queenies from the fish room as well as several heavy dredges to lighten the wreck. Then, airbags were attached, and the *Solway Harvester* was returned to an upright position on the seabed. With the starboard side now visible, it could be inspected for damage, and none was found other than what had been caused by impact with the seabed. Several watertight hatches were also found to be in the open position, as were some of the *Solway Harvester's* internal doors, several of which had been tied open.

Bad weather delayed the recovery operation, but by early February an attempt was made to raise the *Solway Harvester* to the surface. But this failed, with the vessel slipping from its sling and falling several metres to the seabed, damaging the rudder and propeller. A second attempt, the next day, was successful in raising the vessel off the seabed, but the *Solway Harvester* was not lifted to the surface. Instead, due to worsening weather conditions, it was moved to the sheltered Laxley Bay on the east coast of the Isle of Man and lowered back to the seabed. Three divers were then sent to the wreck and successfully recovered all seven bodies of the crew, transferring them to the CSO *Well Servicer*. The recovery operation was then suspended. The bodies of the crewmembers were transported to Douglas, the capital of the Isle of Man. Postmortems were carried out and showed that all died of drowning.

Safety Bulletin Issued and Conspiracy Theories

While the MAIB had already started a full official investigation, this would take months to complete, and it would be well over a year before it was ready to publish. But it was essential to get information about what caused the *Solway Harvester* to sink out to fishing boat owners and skippers as soon as possible. A safety bulletin was therefore prepared for release on 23 February 2000, just forty-three days after the *Solway Harvester* was lost. The introduction of the bulletin stated this was because:

> The MAIB's initial inquiries have revealed evidence of safety shortcomings, which give rise to serious concerns about the safety of all fishing vessels, particularly for the crews sailing on similar scallop dredgers and other trawlers operating out of Kirkcudbright.

The bulletin made three main recommendations. Firstly, the main decks should be checked for watertight integrity, with the bulletin highlighting that one of the scuttle hatches of the *Solway Harvester* was open and had not been fitted with a cover. Secondly, as the *Solway Harvester*'s life rafts had failed to properly release and inflate, the life rafts of all fishing vessels should be checked to ensure they were correctly stored so they would deploy and inflate if the ship began to sink. Finally, with there being no evidence that four of the seven crew of the *Solway Harvester* had the required safety training, the owners and operators of all fishing vessels were urged to ensure that all of their crews had received all necessary training.

But there was another reason that the MAIB saw getting the bulletin released as critically important – speculation that another vessel was involved in the sinking of the *Solway Harvester* was beginning to grow. An article in the Scottish newspaper the *Daily Record* alleged that accident investigators had given a tip-off to senior figures in the Scottish fishing community informing them that the wreck of the *Solway Harvester* showed damage near its bow which was consistent with a collision with a large vessel. It was suggested that this could have been the Royal Navy nuclear-powered submarine HMS *Vanguard*, which returned to Faslane Naval Base allegedly for emergency repairs, three days after the *Solway Harvester* sank. The *Daily Record* claimed that a source who was close to the enquiry told the newspaper that it "Feels as though there is a cover-up going on. The way the information is coming out doesn't sound right … The MoD say they were not even in the Irish Sea at the time but it isn't the first time they have denied any involvement in an incident like this."

Another theory was that the *Solway Harvester* had collided with a shipping container which had been lost from a cargo vessel. Such containers could be up to 12 metres (40 ft) long and weigh four tons and can pose a threat to ships when they are lost overboard as they lie low in the waterline and are difficult to spot. There was some evidence to back up this theory as hundreds of plastic tubs of margarine and mayonnaise had washed up across the coastline of northwest England in the weeks before the *Solway Harvester* was lost, presumably having spilt from a lost shipping container.

In the safety bulletin, the conspiracy theories were decisively ruled out. It was stated that the damage to the wreck of the *Solway Harvester* was consistent with impacting the seabed and there was no damage to the vessel that suggested it had either collided with another vessel or a submarine had snagged its nets. The shipping container theory was also ruled out.

The margarine and mayonnaise tubs had indeed come from a shipping container. They had been lost by the cargo ship MV *Coastal Bay* when it encountered bad weather in October 1999 and four containers slipped from its deck. However, the MAIB stated that the containers had all been accounted for and there was no connection between the MV *Coastal Bay* incident and the loss of the *Solway Harvester*. With this, the conspiracy theories surrounding *Solway Harvester* dissipated, and attention turned to finding out the true cause of the disaster.

Recovery and Examination of the Wreck

In June 2000, the heavy lifting vessel *Norma* was used to recover the wreck of the *Solway Harvester* to the surface, where it was then towed on the surface to the port of Ramsay on the Isle of Man by the Laxley Towing Company, a marine salvage company. The recovery had been funded by the Isle of Man government, which had spent around £1 million on the operation. This led to anger within Scottish communities who said that both the Westminster and Scottish governments had failed to provide funding for the recovery operation, leading to the five-month delay between the *Solway Harvester* being transported to Laxley Bay and then being refloated. Furthermore, it was claimed that local people affected by the disaster had not been supported. A BBC article from 2000 quoted local councillor Douglas Swan as saying:

> If it had been left to the Scottish Executive or the Westminster Parliament the bodies would still have been lying at the bottom of the sea. We have not heard anything from the Scottish government or Westminster ... The UK Government has been dithering about.

With the wreck now recovered, MAIB investigators, the Isle of Man authorities, and representatives of the *Solway Harvester*'s insurers began their respective investigations of the wreck. The *Solway Harvester*'s mate, who had missed the final voyage due to illness, was also brought to the Isle of Man to provide insight into the operation of the vessel.

MAIB investigators examined the wreck in detail to ascertain as much information as possible about the *Solway Harvester* and what caused the vessel to sink. While the *Solway Harvester* had been making its way to Ramsay and was not dredging when it sank, the wreck's analysis revealed that the engine was not engaged and the propeller was de-clutched. This was considered extremely strange as the vessel would have been drifting, exacerbating the effects of the wind and weather and causing much more rolling than proceeding forward under power.

Both the port and starboard ice scuttle hatches were found to be open, with the watertight cover for one found piled amongst loose fishing gear on the main deck and the other completely missing. The watertight bulkheads, fitted by Deeside Marine in 1997 to allow the vessel to meet stability requirements, were also found not to be watertight, with gaps around the areas where pipes passed through the bulkheads. The series of pumps which were relied upon to keep the fish room clear of water were found to be in poor condition. The two pumps suffered from corrosion, incorrect parts being fitted, burnt-out circuits and clogged filters, and the main engine-driven pump for the bilge was damaged to such an extent that it did not work, although the auxiliary backup pump which replaced it did function adequately.

Even if the crew had managed to escape as the *Solway Harvester* sank, the life rafts would not have been available to them. The life rafts should have detached from the vessel and then deployed from their canisters and automatically inflated. Although they did detach, due to being stored improperly they did not inflate, explaining how the two unopened life raft canisters were found on the surface during the search for survivors. Furthermore, both life rafts were supposed to receive an annual service, but there was no evidence they had been serviced since September 1996. While the life rafts did contain the full complement of emergency equipment, the rations were out of date, and the distress flares had expired in August 1998.

Analysis of the Wreck and Further Investigations

With collision theories ruled out and the only damage to the vessel caused by colliding with the seabed, the MAIB began to investigate the extent to which water entered the fish room, believing that if a large amount of water flowed into the fish room, the stability of the *Solway Harvester* could have become compromised. Several experiments were carried out to test this. One test, at a specialist marine research facility in Hampshire, used a one-fifteenth scale model of the *Solway Harvester* and subjected it to various wave and weather conditions. It was found that if the fish room was flooded with water, and the waves and sea conditions were worse than normal, the vessel could capsize, although it would take around eighteen tons of water to flood into the fish room to cause this to happen. However, if the bagged scallops and spare metal dredges stored in the fish room moved 2 metres (6 ft) to either side, the amount of water necessary to cause a capsize was reduced to nine tons.

Further computer analysis of the *Solway Harvester*'s stability was carried out at the University of Strathclyde's Ship Stability Research Centre in the spring and summer of 2001. Computer simulations of the vessel's final hours were used to analyse how wind and wave conditions would interact with the flooding of the fish room and the vessel's rolling to produce the conditions which led to the disaster. Further full-scale tests were carried out on the wreck of the *Solway Harvester*, which included examining how the filled scallop bags and spare dredges could have moved around inside the fish room to destabilize the vessel further, and at-sea tests were also carried out on the *Tobrach-N*.

But just as the MAIB investigation was completed and being readied for release in February 2002, an unexpected turn of events would see its publication delayed by several years.

Criminal Trial

As the MAIB prepared to publish their investigation, the Attorney General of the Isle of Man asked for the release date to be delayed. This was because the government of the Isle of Man was considering taking legal action against the *Solway Harvester*'s owner, Richard Gidney, and believed the report's publication could prejudice a future trial. This could happen as the *Solway Harvester* had sunk within the territorial waters of the Isle of Man, meaning that it fell within the jurisdiction of the island's government. In an exceptionally rare move, the MAIB agreed to delay the publication of the investigation, clearing the way for the legal action to proceed. In June 2002, Gidney was charged with the manslaughter of the seven crew members of the *Solway Harvester*.

The trial started in April 2005, over five years after the disaster. It was held at the Isle of Man's Court of General Gaol Delivery – the equivalent of England and Wales's Crown Court or Scotland's High Court. An article in the *Herald* stated that the trial was expected to last between six and eight weeks, with a jury of eight men and four women being sworn in. Deemster Andrew Moran QC (deemster is the term used for judges in the Isle of Man) would preside over the trial, and over one hundred witnesses had been called, although only one third of them would give evidence.

For five weeks, the prosecution outlined their case, alleging that the vessel was operating with a series of known safety issues and technical faults, with the missing scuttle hatch cover, broken bilge alarm and malfunctioning pumps being highlighted as especially serious issues. In an article in the *Guardian*, Gidney was quoted as saying that he had not been aware of the many safety issues with the *Solway Harvester*, saying he had "not received any reports of the pumps not working" and if he had he would have ordered a new one.

He also denied that he had been informed about the persistent flooding of the fish room in the months before the disaster, again claiming that he would have addressed this if he had been told about it. Gidney went on to say that Craig Mills, as the skipper, was responsible for all aspects of safety on board the *Solway Harvester* and was quoted in the same *Guardian* article as saying:

> The company delegated responsibility for all health and safety matters to the skippers. The skipper was responsible for safety on board the vessel ... He [Craig Mills] never mentioned any defects to me during these meetings.

Gidney's defence put forward the idea of a 'dry capsize.' In this scenario, the *Solway Harvester* sank because bagged scallops and fishing gear moved to one side of the fish room, destabilizing the vessel and causing it to capsize. According to this theory, the amount of water that flooded into the fish room was negligible and did not contribute to the loss of the vessel. The MAIB investigation would, when it was later published, decisively rule out a dry capsize as causing the disaster.

But five weeks into the trial, Deemster Andrew Moran called a halt to proceedings and directed the jury to return a not guilty verdict, clearing Gidney of all charges. He said that Gidney had demonstrated "proactive and safety-conscious" conduct when a flooding incident happened on the *Solway Harvester*'s sister ship, *Tobrach-N*, and there was no way that the evidence being presented in court could lead to a criminal conviction of manslaughter. Moran was quoted in a BBC News article as saying after the trial that the evidence put before the jury was:

> Insufficient to establish that there was any lack of care, particularly regarding what was the common and accepted practice of the vessel. ... I have a duty to stop this case from proceeding any further and I must direct the jury to return verdicts of not guilty.

Many of the family members of the men who lost their lives expressed their anger and dismay over the collapse of the trial, and Reverend Alex

Currie, who had become a spokesperson for the families, told the BBC that he was:

> Devastated that these families have had to wait five years for a resolution, and all in vain. We'd always hoped that a trial would bring some closure to the tragedy ... No one wanted vengeance, just closure - but my initial reaction is that this closure will not now happen.

MAIB Report Finally Published

With the legal action concluded, the MAIB investigation was finally released on 20 January 2006, almost four years later than planned. With the report's publication, the series of events and combination of factors which led to the loss of the *Solway Harvester* could finally be revealed, and the flooding of the fish room was seen as a decisive factor in the loss of the vessel.

The report stated that the *Solway Harvester* was not engaged in fishing when it sank and was heading toward Ramsay Bay on the Isle of Man to shelter from the worsening weather conditions. Due to the missing ice scuttle hatch covers, water had been downflooding into the fish room and continued to do so as the *Solway Harvester* made its way through the Irish Sea. As the alarm which warned of water build up in the fish room, and the system of pumps which removed the water were both broken, water continued to flood into the fish room. None of the crew appeared to have been aware of this until, at around 5.30 pm, it is likely that one of the crew carried out a visual check of the fish room and reported the water level to Craig Mills. By this point, the vessel would have been rolling heavily from side to side, causing many of the 176 bags of scallops and spare dredges (which collectively weighed around two tons) to come loose and move to the starboard side of the fish room, further destabilizing the vessel.

With no mate on board, Mills had no choice other than to disengage the engine and go and deal with the issue himself. This left the *Solway Harvester* drifting and increased its vulnerability to the weather conditions. Mills likely instructed the crew to bail out the water using buckets, but there may have been as much as nine tons of water in the fish room. At approximately 5.45 pm, while in this highly unstable state, the *Solway Harvester* was likely struck by a succession of heavy waves, which caused the vessel to capsize and then rapidly sink beneath the waves.

MAIB Criticisms and 2008 Coroner's Verdict

The MAIB report was highly critical of the condition of the *Solway Harvester.* Safety issues that had been outlined in the emergency bulletin were reiterated – the life rafts were overdue for servicing and had been stored in such a way that they would not inflate once deployed, and several crew members had not undergone mandatory safety training. However, it was the failure to maintain the watertight integrity of the vessel that had been the decisive factor in the disaster, and this received the most attention in the report.

The open ice scuttle hatches were the primary cause of the fish room flooding. The original role of these hatches was to allow scallop meat, which had been removed from its shell by a machine on the deck, to be transferred to the fish room. On the *Solway Harvester,* they were no longer used for this purpose as the scallops gathered by the dredges were taken to the fish room still in their shells. The ice scuttles should, therefore, have been replaced with conventional hatches with watertight covers, which should have remained closed when not in use (which would have been almost all of the time). This did not happen and the ice scuttle hatches were left as they were, and when the covers were lost, they were not replaced, allowing a route for water to downflood into the fish room. This may have been because both the skipper and owner considered the part of the deck where the ice scuttle hatches were located to be mostly dry and believed that only a small amount of water could get through them. They were incorrect in this belief. The MAIB investigation calculated that the equivalent of a bucketful of water could flow down the ice scuttle hatches every sixteen seconds in bad weather. This would lead to the loss of stability becoming dangerous in around seventy-five minutes if the pumps were not functioning and no other action was taken to remove the water.

The report went on to say that the flooding of the fish room was not seen as a particularly serious issue by either Andrew Mills or Richard Gidney. It was not discussed during their regular meetings, which usually focused on the profitability and catch levels of the *Solway Harvester*. Mills likely thought that the pumping system, when combined with periodic checks from crewmembers, was an adequate way of managing the flooding, and when there was excess water due to the pumps not working, it could be removed using buckets. The previous flooding incidents had not led to any serious consequences with both Mills and the crew seeing them as more of an inconvenience that impacted their ability to make good catches rather than a threat to the safety of the vessel. The MAIB report went on to say that in a "perverse way", the previous flooding incidents, "probably … increased their confidence in *Solway Harvester* and her ability to survive in any conditions." The MAIB said that while Mills, like Gidney who skippered the *Solway Harvester* before him, had the required qualifications and experience for the role of skipper, there was no evidence that they had any knowledge of the risks to stability and buoyancy of fishing vessels, and neither appeared to be aware that water flooding into the fish room could threaten the stability of the entire vessel.

The large size of the fish room, which stretched across the entire breadth of the *Solway Harvester* and along more than a third of its length, was also seen as a contributing factor. Due to the size of the room, a large amount of water could build up, but would only cover a shallow depth, leading the crew to disregard how serious this was and the impact it had on the vessel's stability. Furthermore, the large size of the room meant that it was used to store additional equipment, such as the spare dredges which came loose and contributed to the *Solway Harvester* losing stability.

The faulty bilge alarm was highlighted as another major factor in the sinking. With no alarm in the fish room, the skipper had no way of knowing the water level there and had to rely on crewmembers carrying out visual checks and then reporting back to him. The report stated that if the alarm had been working it was highly likely the disaster would not have happened, as even if the pumping system had not been working, Mills would have sent his crew out much earlier to bail out the water with buckets and maintained the stability of the *Solway Harvester*. The MAIB report decisively stated that the overall condition of the *Solway Harvester* was so poor that "had MCA [Maritime and Coastguard Agency] surveyors inspected *Solway Harvester* on the day she sank, there were enough shortcomings for her to be detained."

In 2008, a coroner officially recorded a verdict of accidental death on the seven crewmembers who died on board the *Solway Harvester*, finally ending the legal process after almost nine years. Despite this verdict, Coroner Michael Moyle was highly critical of Richard Gidney, who had only given evidence when a court order compelled him to do so. Michael Moyle said:

> Certain parts of Mr Gidney's evidence I found to be unsatisfactory or inadequate. Mr Gidney had concluded his evidence by endeavouring to dispel any suggestion that the Solway Harvester was not properly maintained or properly equipped. Many others, myself included, might not necessarily share such a view.

Other Vessels Owned by Richard Gidney and the *St Amant* Accident

Several other vessels owned by Richard Gidney have been involved in controversial incidents. In February 2000, less than two months after the loss of the *Solway Harvester*, two vessels owned by Richard Gidney's company, the dredgers *St Keverne* and the *Karianda,* were detained at Mallaig on the west coast of the Scottish Highlands by the MCA after serious safety issues were found on both vessels. A spokesperson for the MCA said that the watertight integrity of the main deck of the vessels had been "compromised" with the same issue which caused the loss of the *Solway Harvester*. Other issues included "faulty seals on hatches, out-of-date escape hatch clips and navigation charts, and fire extinguishers in need of servicing." The vessels were eventually released.

Six months later, the *Karianda* sank while fishing in calm conditions in the North Sea off the coast of Stonehaven, Aberdeenshire. The crew did not issue a distress call but were rescued from their life raft by helicopter after they activated an emergency beacon. The reason for the sinking of the vessel remains mysterious, with a report in the *Herald* newspaper claiming that one of the crewmembers said that he was instructed to deliberately sink the ship by burning a hole in the hull using a blowtorch. No further information on the *Karianda* or subsequent events regarding its loss has been made public.

In 2012, the 18 metre (59 ft) long, 57-ton dredger, *St Amant*, which was part-owned by Richard Gidney, was sailing from the port of Holyhead in Wales, heading to shellfish beds in Cardigan Bay. At an unknown time, likely around 1.00 am, 25-year-old deckhand Steven Robinson was lost overboard, although the rest of the crew were not aware until approximately one hour later. Robinson was not wearing a personal floatation device or locator beacon when he fell and was dressed in only a T-shirt and jeans. A thorough search, which involved police and Royal Air Force helicopters, Royal National Lifeboat Institution lifeboats, fishing boats and commercial ships, was initiated, but Robinson could not be located. His body has never been found.

The MAIB investigated this incident and concluded that Robinson fell overboard while on the deck to urinate over the side of the ship. He was doing this because the toilet the vessel had originally been fitted with had been removed and was never replaced. The MAIB found that a significant contributory factor was that the deck walls were lower than the required height. There were multiple other issues with the safety and hygiene on board the *St Amant*. An inspection found that the crew had not been briefed on safety procedures, and multiple repeat inspections found that no attempts had been made to rectify this. Equipment such as hoses and spare dredges were stored on the deck contrary to regulations and the vessel had no facilities to refrigerate food despite the crew being at sea for up to ten days at a time. The only sink at which the crew could wash themselves was in the galley, and it was also found that in bad weather, the crew would use a bucket in the fish hold – where the fish they had caught and their own supply of food was stored – as a toilet. It was concluded that "the skipper and crewmen had an extremely poor attitude to establishing and maintaining a safe working environment on board the vessel", and conditions on board were "unacceptable for commercial fishermen in the twenty-first century to have to live and work in." The following year, a coroner ruled that Robinson's death was an accident, saying, "I fail to find a degree of negligence so gross it becomes criminal."

Solway Harvester Dismantled and Memorials to the Disaster

The *Solway Harvester* remained moored at the port in Douglas until 2013 when, following the investigations and legal action being concluded, permission was given for the vessel to be disposed of. Laxley Towing Company, which had assisted in the salvage of the vessel after the disaster, began the process of dismantling the *Solway Harvester*, completing the process in January 2014. Steven Carter, from the company, told the BBC that the presence of the ship had been a "sad and macabre reminder" of the tragedy "for long enough", and he hoped the removal of the vessel would bring closure.

There are two memorials to the *Solway Harvesters* at the Isle of Whithorn in Scotland, the town where the crew came from. One consists of an anchor on top of a boulder with the names of the seven crewmembers carved underneath. The other is a plinth which contains text thanking the Isle of Man community for their help and support in the disaster, with the flags of the Isle of Man and Scotland pictured below. On 11 January 2020, the Scottish and Isle of Man communities came together to commemorate the twentieth anniversary of the disaster at a service at St Ninians's Priory Church in Whithorn.

Chapter 9

The 1914 Newfoundland Sealing Disasters

In March 1914, hundreds of men departed ships which had broken through the ice fields of Newfoundland to catch and kill harp seals. But a terrible storm would set in, causing heavy rain, snowfall and wild seas. Two separate disasters would take place simultaneously and the people of Newfoundland would eventually discover that 251 men had lost their lives.

History of Sealing in Newfoundland

Newfoundland is a large island off the eastern coast of North America. In 1914, the year of the disasters, it was a self-governing dominion of the British Empire (it did not become a part of Canada until 1949). The subarctic climate of Newfoundland means that during the late winter and spring, ice sheets begin to form and extend outward from the island's coastline, only receding as the temperature rises in the late spring and early summer. A wide variety of wildlife can be found across Newfoundland, including caribou (wild reindeer), polar bears, arctic foxes, arctic hares, a wide range of marine birds and several species of seals.

First Nations people began hunting seals on a subsistence basis in Newfoundland thousands of years ago, but the first commercial seal hunting began with the arrival of Europeans in the 1500s. Just as cod were caught, preserved by salting, and then taken back to Europe to be sold, seal skins and oil derived from seal fat were also transported to Europe. With seals being abundant across the vast ice fields and ice floes of Newfoundland, this soon became a profitable industry for the Europeans.

Large-scale seal hunting began in the mid-1700s. Sail-powered schooners would traverse the ice-covered waters of Newfoundland and hunt the abundant seals. Hundreds of schooners descended on Newfoundland in the early spring months, killing hundreds of thousands of seals each year. But the wooden schooners were limited by wind and weather conditions, and if the ice was thick, they could only catch seals on the outer ice fields. Sealing, nevertheless, became a highly lucrative industry. The meat of seals was widely eaten, the skin was used for clothing and seal oil was used as lamp oil, in cooking and in the production of soap, lipstick and margarine.

Sealing, like many other types of commercial fishing, was transformed by the advent of steam power in the mid-1800s. Steam-powered sealing vessels were not restricted by the wind and could handle sea conditions which would have wrecked wooden schooners. Steamers could push further into the ice fields, opening up new, previously inaccessible, areas to sealing. Although they were still primarily made out of wood, steam-powered vessels were much larger than schooners, meaning they could carry more seals back home. This larger size also allowed steamers to carry more supplies and stay out at sea for longer, and larger crews meant men could work in shifts, allowing seals to be hunted for much longer periods of time.

The power and efficiency of steam-powered vessels meant that the smaller schooners soon became uneconomical to operate and rapidly reduced in number as steamers came to dominate the Newfoundland sealing industry. But by the late 1800s, wooden steamers were becoming outdated as they were replaced by newer, steel-hulled vessels. While these were also powered by steam engines, they were able to act as ice breakers, smashing through ice which would have been impassable for the wooden-hulled ships they replaced. But the greater efficiency of these vessels meant fewer were needed to catch the required number of seals. The sealing industry, which had directly employed 10,000 men across hundreds of ships in the mid-1800s, only employed between 3,000 and 4,000 men across twenty vessels by the turn of the century.

The Sealing Fleet of 1914

In mid-March 1914, the twenty ships of the Newfoundland sealing fleet left the harbour at the city of St John's on the southeastern tip of the island, steaming to the ice fields to begin the sealing season. The wooden-hulled steamers the *Kite, Diana, Southern Cross* and *Newfoundland* – the smallest, oldest and slowest ships in the fleet – departed first. A day later, the faster steel-hulled ships left St John's. These ships – the *Florizel, Bellaventure*, and *Beothic* along with several others – were all built in the twentieth century and were substantially larger and more capable than the wooden ships. The most powerful ship of them all was the *Stephano*. It was built in 1911 in Glasgow and was almost 100 metres (325 ft) in length with a gross tonnage of 3,449 tons. It was captained by 58-year-old Abram Kean, a man whose fearsome reputation and decades of sealing experience had earned him the unofficial title of the admiral of the sealing fleet. Historian Melvin Baker describes his reputation:

> [Abram Kean] was senior captain for Bowring Brothers [the company which owned the *Stephano*], one of Newfoundland's largest fish businesses. … This position allowed him to exert great influence on public opinion … He was a man of supreme confidence in his seafaring abilities who commanded the largest and most powerful vessels at the seal fishery.

Baker went on to say that while Abram Kean had a reputation as a harsh and unforgiving captain, who demanded the utmost effort and commitment from his men, this did not put people off from working with him. Almost all of the men looking for a place on a sealing boat would choose Abram Kean above all others, such was his reputation for seal hunting and returning home with the most profitable catches.

Abram Kean's two sons were also captaining sealing ships in the fleet. His oldest son, 41-year-old Joseph Kean, commanded the fleet's second largest ship, the 93 metre (305 ft) steel-hulled *Florizel*, while 29-year-old Westbury Kean captained the 64 metre (212 ft) long, ageing, wooden *Newfoundland*.

Arriving at the Ice

The sealing season was short, lasting between four and six weeks across March and April each year. This was because the species of seals which were being hunted – harp seals – are migratory. They spend the summer in the Arctic waters of northern Canada and Greenland, swimming south thousands of miles over the winter and arrive at Newfoundland in the early spring. Once there, the female harp seals give birth on the ice. The newly born seal pups are weak and immobile and remain on the ice, being nursed by their mothers and putting on weight at the rate of 5 lbs (2.2 kg) per day. But this stage of their lives only lasts a short time. Within weeks the white fur of the seals begins to be replaced by coarser grey fur, and they soon enter the water and begin to hunt fish species such as cod, American plaice and immature halibut. These pups, known as whitecoats because of the soft, white fur which covered their bodies, were the target of the sealers, and the sealing fleet only had a limited window of time in which to make their catches.

J.S. Colman, writing in 1949, explained how fully-grown harp seals, and other seal species, such as hood seals, were mostly ignored by the sealers:

> The prime object of the hunt is the baby harps of 'whitecoats' during the first three weeks after birth; at this stage they not only lie helpless on the ice and are easily killed, but are covered with a valuable coat of white wool.

He went on the say that the coarse coats of the adult harp seals were much less valuable, and the oil they produced was of a lower quality. Hood seals were more aggressive, making them harder to catch and the young could swim almost from birth, meaning there were fewer opportunities to catch them as pups. Overall harp seals made up 90 per cent of all seal catches.

The steel ships soon caught up with the wooden steamers and as the entire fleet approached the ice fields the search for seals began. Owned by the Newfoundland Sealing Company, the 65 m (212 ft) long *Newfoundland* was built in 1872 and was powered by a steam engine built at Ouseburn Engine Works in Newcastle upon Tyne, England. It had once been one of the most capable vessels in the fleet but was now outdated, and outclassed by the steel ships in almost every aspect. The winter of 1914 had been colder than usual, and the loose ice sheets of the previous season, which the *Newfoundland* had been able to traverse, were now almost impassable for the ship. Ice surrounded the *Newfoundland*, becoming thicker and progressively more difficult to move through as they grew closer to the ice sheets. While the steel-hulled ships moved further into the distance, the *Newfoundland*, along with the *Kite* and *Diana* fell behind. Westbury Kean had to send his men out of the ship where they used hammers and axes to smash a pathway in the ice to allow their ship to move forward. It was backbreaking work, often carried out knee-deep in freezing water and the crew of the *Newfoundland* could take an entire day just to move their ship forward a few miles.

Westbury Kean was also under pressure. As the son of the renowned Abram Kean, he was expected to return with his ship full of seal pelts, even if the *Newfoundland* was an old and outdated sealing vessel. His older brother, Joseph, had already performed well and had been promoted to the steel-hulled *Florizel*. Westbury had no excuses – he was expected to replicate his brother's and father's successes.

Sealing captains had total authority on board their ships, but they were effectively employees who were appointed to the role by the companies which owned the vessels. These companies ran the sealing ships as a ruthless money-making enterprise. Under Newfoundland law at the time, there were practically no rules or regulations in place to protect the welfare of the men on the sealing ships. The sealing companies had no obligation to issue crews with clothes capable of protecting them from the harsh and freezing environment or supply any other safety equipment. Little training took place, with the new sealers relying on informal instructions from the more experienced men on board.

While the ships operated as a fleet and would work together to locate seal colonies, they were simultaneously competing against each other, with the captains' reputations being almost entirely based on the number of seal pelts they returned to port with. The smaller ships, which would not stay out as long as the larger steel-hulled vessels due to their holds reaching their capacity sooner, would instead compete for the prestige of being the first ship of the season to return to St John's full of seal pelts. But for the larger vessels, the aim was to stay out at sea for as long as possible and return with as many seal pelts as they could.

Returning home with a hold full to capacity with seal pelts meant good profits for the companies which owned the vessels. The captain and officers, already paid a good wage by the standards of the time, would also receive bonuses if catch targets were reached. The lowest paid were the men who went out onto the ice to carry out the sealing. But sealing still paid more than the cod fishing or logging work that provided employment for the rest of the year, explaining why so many were so keen to be on board the sealing vessels despite the conditions and danger they faced.

Sealing Begins

As the *Newfoundland* made slow progress through the ice, the steel-hulled vessels were already deep in the ice fields and had found a colony of harp seals. The first seal hunt of the season began as men were sent out over the sides of their ships and onto the ice. While steam power had allowed new areas to be accessed, the work the men carried out on the ice had changed little since the age of sail power. The men would often have to walk many miles over ice sheets that often consisted of rough, serrated ice which had to be clambered over while carrying their equipment. Thin sheet ice could crack or collapse underfoot without warning, leaving the men, who typically wore woollen clothing and canvas jackets, soaked through in sub-zero temperatures. This meant that once on the ice, the sealing teams could end up miles away from their ship, and were vulnerable to being caught in storms, or become further separated from their ship if the ice sheet they were on began to drift out to sea. Fog, snowstorms and heavy rain could quickly descend on an area and reduce visibility to almost zero. Sealing ships often had to repeatedly sound their steam whistle (which was powered by the boiler), and the sealers on the ice relied on hearing this sound to find their way back to their ship. Photokeratitis, better known as snow blindness, was another issue which affected sealers. This was damage caused to sealers' eyes when ultraviolet rays from the sun reflected off the brilliant white snow. Symptoms include the eyes becoming painful, red, swollen and increasingly sensitive to light, but by the start of the twentieth century, goggles were available to some sealers which afforded some protection from snow blindness, although few men in the Newfoundland sealing fleet had access to these.

When the seals were reached the men would kill the helpless whitecoats by striking them on the head or nose with gaffs – long poles with metal hooks fastened to the end – killing the baby seals instantly. In the book *Death on the Ice*, which covers the disaster, Cassie Brown writes that many of the men found it hard to kill the baby seals the first time they went onto the ice, but abuse and jeering from their more experienced colleagues soon made them toughen up and carry out the task of killing baby seals.

Once the whitecoats had been killed the sealers would use razor-sharp knives to remove the pelts (the skin and the attached fat), which were then left in a pile, marked by a flag to show which ship they belonged to. Often, after a large group of seals had been killed and skinned, the ice would flow red with blood. The sealers would then move on to further groups of seals, working their way back to collect the piles of pelts as they returned to their ships. Having the pelts stolen by the sealers of another boat, or the flag being swapped with that of another ship, was a constant risk, although one in which crews from all ships took part. By the twentieth century, seal meat was rarely eaten and was of little value – only the pelt was retained, and the rest of the seal was simply left on the ice. If seals were plentiful, multiple teams from a sealing ship could collectively kill many thousands of whitecoat seals in a single day.

Just as the crews were badly equipped in terms of clothing, conditions on even the most modern sealing ships soon deteriorated as the sealing season progressed. There was simply no way to keep the ships clean once tens of thousands of bloody seal pelts started to be taken on board. The men, covered in blood, fat and grease from sealing, had few ways of cleaning themselves on board, and most simply accepted that they would be filthy and stinking for the majority of their time at sea, living on limited food in terrible conditions. As the writer Harold Horwood describes:

> The men had no meals to cook … for weeks and months they lived on sea biscuits and tea. Even their drinking water was polluted with blood … As the pelts and fat piled up, they simply lived on top of their cargo in the utter filth.

The *Newfoundland* finds the *Stephano*

The *Stephano*, *Beothic* and *Florizel* had all found seals and had men out on the ice killing seals and collecting pelts. Soon thousands of seal pelts were safely stored away in their holds, but they would need to have tens of thousands more for the season to be considered a success. The relatively small colony of seals they had found had been completely depleted and the steel ships began to prepare to move on and find the main colony, which they knew could not be far away.

At 45 metres (146 ft) in length and a gross tonnage of 520 tons, the *Southern Cross* was one of the smallest vessels in the fleet. Despite being a wooden vessel, it had managed to find seals, and due to its small size, had already filled its hold. It therefore set off back to St John's, its captain, George Clarke, keen to gain the prestige and honour of being the first ship to return from the season's seal hunt. The situation was very different for the other wooden ships, the *Kite*, *Diana* and *Newfoundland*. They were still making slow progress through the edge of the ice fields and had only sent men out to hunt small, isolated groups of seals they came across. Westbury Kean, on the *Newfoundland*, needed to find a large colony of seals if he was to avoid the 1914 season from turning into a complete disaster, and have further doubt cast on his ability to live up to his father's reputation.

The *Stephano* led the steel ships and pushed further into the ice field, the crew and officers looking intently for signs of the main seal colony through their binoculars and telescopes. They did not have to search for long. As they moved forward the colony – more than half a mile wide and several miles long – appeared ahead of them. Abram Kean sent his men over the side of the boat. The other steel ships soon arrived on the scene, with their men following the *Stephano*'s onto the ice.

It was 8.00 am on 31 March when Westbury Kean on the *Newfoundland* looked across the ice and saw the outlines of the *Stephano* and *Florizel*, the vessels captained by his father and older brother, several miles away on the other side of the vast ice field. But he was not able to speak to his father or brother. While the steel ships were fitted with wireless radio sets which allowed the captains to communicate with each other, the wireless radio which had previously been fitted to the *Newfoundland* had recently been removed by the vessel's owners. They had decided that, as it had not increased seal catches, it was nothing more than an unnecessary expense, and it was therefore stripped from the vessel. Westbury Kean and his father had devised a much more rudimentary way of communicating with each other. As Westbury observed the *Stephano* from across the ice field through his telescope he saw the vessel's aft crane raise upwards – the sign from his father that they had found seals.

One hundred and sixty-six men prepared to leave the *Newfoundland* to cross the ice field and kill and gather the seals his father had found. They would be led by the ship's second-in-command. The 32-year-old George Tuff was a highly experienced sealer, having been going onto the ice since he was a teenager and had steadily worked his way up the ranks to become a senior officer on board the *Newfoundland*. He had been involved in the *Greenland* sealing ship disaster of 1898 where over one hundred men had been put on the ice, but bad weather set in and prevented their ship from returning to collect them, forcing the men to stay on the ice overnight. When the *Greenland* could reach them the next day, forty-eight of the men were dead. George Tuff, then aged just seventeen, was one of the survivors, but as Cassie Brown writes in *Death on the Ice* "the horror never quite left Tuff."

Westbury Kean instructed Tuff to take his men across the miles of ice sheet and go directly to the *Stephano*. There he should ask Abram Kean to be directed to the seal colony. If the seals were plentiful, which Westbury Kean very much hoped they would be, the men would be working on the ice for many hours. Believing the journey back to the *Newfoundland* was too far for the men to travel after a day of sealing, Westbury Kean told George Tuff not to return to the *Newfoundland* after the sealing was complete, and instead go to the *Stephano* and stay on his father's ship for the night. Tuff, who was busy preparing equipment and briefing his men, would later testify that he did not hear this order.

The weather was calm and, for Newfoundland on the last day of March, relatively mild, but the clouds overhead were darkening. The *Newfoundland* was equipped with only the most basic of barometers and no thermometer, meaning the crew had no way of accurately predicting how the weather would change. Some of the more experienced crewmembers warned that the dark clouds a were sign that heavy snow or rain was coming, but Westbury Kean was not going to call off the seal hunt based on a weather prediction which may prove incorrect.

The men went over the side of the ship and onto the ice, many of the younger men excited to take part in their first proper seal hunt. The men marched forward, but the going was difficult. The ice they were traversing consisted of high ridges and broken, hard ground, and it took great effort to make progress. They encountered small groups of seals, with a few of the men breaking away to make kills, but above them, the clouds continued to darken and the wind grew in strength. Some of the men became concerned, and a group of thirty-four turned back to the *Newfoundland*, much to the derision of the majority of the men who continued across the ice.

At the same time, as the men from the *Newfoundland* were starting their journey across the ice, the *Southern Cross* made its way through the Labrador Sea, heading back to the harbour at St John's with its hold full of seal pelts. But the darkening clouds were a sign that a storm was indeed on the way, moving across the Grand Banks where it would soon reach the city of St John's. From there, it would move along the coast of Newfoundland and close in on their location. But George Clark, captaining the *Southern Cross*, continued onward, determined to be the first captain of the season to return home.

Reaching the *Stephano* and Sealing on the Ice

After four hours of trekking over the ice, the men from the *Newfoundland* reached the *Stephano*. They were brought on board and given bread and butter to eat and tea to drink. The *Stephano*'s captain, Abram Kean, then told George Tuff that his men would not be spending the night on board the ship. Instead, he would steam southwest and drop them on the ice in the middle of the seal colony. There, they would be able to catch thousands of seals. As they would be dropped just two miles away from the *Newfoundland* they would easily be able to make it back before darkness set in, and as the *Newfoundland* was trapped in the ice, there was no danger it would move away. Abram Kean also told Tuff that he was confident that the weather would not get any worse. George Tuff was subordinate to any sealing ship captain and was in absolutely no position to question a direct order from the admiral of the entire sealing fleet. He, therefore, accepted Abram Kean's instructions without question.

Tuff and the *Newfoundland* men were dropped back on the ice a short while after boarding the *Stephano*. Many of the men were concerned about the weather. When they had boarded the *Stephano*, the *Newfoundland* was distant but still visible. In the short time they had been on board the steel ship, the weather had worsened significantly, and the falling snow made it impossible to see the *Newfoundland*. Many feared they would be unable to find their ship and risked becoming stranded on the ice. Others were unaware that the plan had changed, and still believed that they would be returning to the *Stephano* and spending the night there.

The storm continued to move toward Newfoundland and soon reached St John's. The heavy snowfall set in as the city was battered by winds which caused tiles to fly from roofs and branches to be snapped from trees. The *Southern Cross* had still not arrived, but no one in St John's was overly concerned. Most people assumed that the captain would have sought shelter from the storm in St Mary's Bay further along the coast, and it was only a matter of time before a message came through with news that the ship was safe. But like the *Newfoundland*, the *Southern Cross* had no wireless radio on board, and there was no way of directly contacting the ship.

Back on the ice, the *Newfoundland* men found the main seal colony and killed a small number of seals, but the weather conditions were steadily deteriorating as the storm began to reach them, and they soon abandoned the sealing to – as ordered by Abram Kean – head back to their ship. Snow swirled all around the men, reducing visibility to near zero as the cold winds grew stronger and stronger. Even though the weather was worsening, George Tuff believed that there was no cause for concern. It would be difficult and uncomfortable but with just a few miles to cover he was confident the men would be back on board the *Newfoundland* before darkness set in.

Lost on the Ice

The *Newfoundland* men continued forward slowly, making their way across the ice through the biting wind and heavy snow. They believed they were following the same course that they had taken to the *Stephano* that morning, and simply had to retrace their steps to reach their ship. But the ice was no easier to cross than it had been on the way to the

Stephano, with the men having to scramble over ridges as the ice moved beneath their feet. Some sections of ice gave way, dropping the men into the arctic waters below, where they had to be dragged out by their colleagues. The storm had now reached blizzard conditions with snow, rain and freezing winds lashing the men, freezing their hands and feet and turning their faces bright red with frostbite.

The men struggled on, but even though they believed they were within a mile of the *Newfoundland* it became clear that the men could not continue. As freezing, exhausted and ill-equipped as they were, they would have to spend the night on the ice, although they hoped that when they failed to return, search teams would be sent out to look for them, with many believing it was perfectly possible that they could be rescued before sunrise. Tuff gave the order for the men to gather ice blocks. After hours of backbreaking work, a wall which provided some shelter from the wind and elements had been constructed from ice. Tuff told his men to take cover behind the wall and the gaffs, ropes and flagpoles were broken up and used as firewood. Snow was melted for drinking water and what meagre food the men had, mostly hard tack (a type of biscuit made of flour and water), was eaten. The temperature (with the windchill factor taken into account) reached -20 °C (-4.0 °F), freezing the men, who had no choice other than to shelter behind their ice wall and try to survive the night. To fall asleep would almost certainly result in death. The men had to constantly stand up and move, as only by staying active would they keep their bodies warm enough to survive. The Commission of Enquiry, which was published in 1915 after the disaster, described how the shelter the men had made did offer some protection from the elements, but after an hour the wind changed direction, negating the shelter it offered, and, as the night progressed,

> The cold increased and the storm raged fiercely throughout the whole of that night and into the next day. Before morning several deaths had occurred, principally amongst those who had fallen into the water on the previous day and had remained throughout in wet or frozen clothing.

The following morning it became clear that many had not survived the night. The number of dead was impossible to determine, as heavy snowfall and snowdrifts had covered many of the bodies, but those that could be found were left where they had died, their bodies frozen solid. The exhausted, freezing survivors staggered to their feet and prepared themselves to continue onward. As terrible as the night had been, the men believed they could soon cover the mile which they believed lay between their location and the safety of the *Newfoundland*.

Concerns Grow

On the *Stephano*, Abram Kean was confident that the men on the ice would have safely made their way back to their ship, but on the *Newfoundland*, his son, Westbury Kean was not as sure. Doubts were starting to creep into his mind as he began to wonder if George Tuff had fully comprehended his instruction to stay on board the *Stephano* that night. But it was unthinkable that the men had been stuck on the ice overnight somewhere between the two ships, and he managed to convince himself that the men had indeed spent the night safe on the *Stephano*. If the wireless radio had still been installed on his ship he would have been able to clear up the situation in minutes, but, with no radio, he simply had to hope that his instructions had been understood and followed. Furthermore, the *Newfoundland* was still stuck in the ice and unable to move. Even if Westbury Kean had wanted to search for his men, he was unable to do so.

Few of the men on the *Stephano* shared Abram Kean's confidence. The crew were highly concerned that the men who had been sent onto the ice would have been unable to reach the *Newfoundland* in the storm conditions and they also believed that Abram Kean had miscalculated his position and dropped the men much further than two miles from the *Newfoundland*. These fears were heightened when Abram Kean's oldest son, Joseph Kean, the captain of the *Florizel*, radioed the *Stephano* and expressed his concern about the *Newfoundland* men. But Abram Kean was seen as infallible, and none of his men, not even his senior officers, could directly challenge him. If he said the *Newfoundland* men had made their way safely back to their own ship, they all had to accept that is what had happened.

By the night of 31 March, the worst of the storm had passed St John's, and the people of the city were assessing the damage that had been caused. But worrying news had reached the city. Earlier that day, the *Portia*, a passenger and mail-carrying ship, reported that it had seen the *Southern Cross*. But the *Portia* had made for St Mary's Bay and the shelter it offered and the *Southern Cross* had not followed and had stayed out at sea, seeming to continue onward toward St John's. If it had made for St John's the *Southern Cross* should certainly have reached the city by now. Fears began to grow, but, with the seas still stormy and rough, ships could not be sent out to search for the *Southern Cross*. With no way of contacting the vessel the people of St John's had no choice other than to wait, and hope the *Southern Cross* eventually returned.

Nearly Rescued and the Second Night on the Ice

The surviving *Newfoundland* men continued to trek onward but they slowly began to realize that they had covered more than a mile and there was no sign of the *Newfoundland*. It began to dawn on the men that Abram Kean was mistaken about where he dropped them on the ice, and they were much further away from their ship than they realised. The men had to accept that the one further mile they thought they had to travel was now a journey of an unknown distance. But they had no choice other than to keep walking. By midday on 1 April, the storm began to ease and visibility improved. It was then that the men believed they had found their salvation. Two and a half miles ahead of them, just off the coast was the *Bellaventure*. A small group of the men pushed forward toward the ship, coming within a quarter of a mile of the vessel, waving flags attached to gaffs to try and gain the attention of the crew. In the 1915 Commission of Enquiry, it is stated that they could see crewmembers working on the deck and hauling seals on board, but the crew of the *Bellaventure* somehow could not see them and after a few minutes, the *Bellaventure* began to sail out to sea.

Only now did the extent of the calamitous miscommunication between Abram Kean, Westbury Kean and George Tuff become clear. The *Bellaventure* was engaged in their normal activity of sealing. They had not set rescue teams down on the ice or sailed parallel to the coastline as they would have done if they were looking for the *Newfoundland* men, and no one on the vessel appeared to be using binoculars or telescopes to look for men on the ice. Westbury Kean thought they had spent the night on the *Stephano*, and Abram Kean thought they had returned to the *Newfoundland*. No one on any ship knew that they were lost on the ice.

The solitary comfort they could take was at least the old, wooden *Newfoundland* was stuck in the ice and was unable to move away from them as the *Bellaventure* had. There was only an hour of daylight left and they redoubled their efforts to reach their ship. A group of ten men, led by George Tuff, pushed forward in the direction of the *Newfoundland*. Others, who were weaker, injured or soaked due to falling into the water lagged behind, trudging slowly through the ice, whereas some men, too weak to move, gave up and collapsed on the ice. If they could not be dragged back onto their feet by their colleagues, death was inevitable.

The group of ten at the front continued forward, the going was still difficult, but the jagged ridges of ice slowly gave way to smoother ice which at least offered some respite and allowed them to save some of their energy. Furthermore, the snow began to lighten as the worst of the storm began to pass. After several more hours, the men slowly made out the shape of the *Newfoundland* around a mile ahead of them. They pressed forward, energised by the belief that they were finally safe, but when they were halfway there the unthinkable happened. The *Newfoundland* finally broke free of the ice and began to steam back out to sea. The group of men, who were, at their closest point, just half an hour away from being back on board had the ship remained stuck in the ice, fell to their knees in despair. Another night on the ice was now inevitable.

126

For the second night, the men, now strung out into smaller groups all across the ice, lacked the energy and coherence to construct any kind of ice shelter. The power of the storm had lessened, but conditions were still harsh. Cassie Brown describes the second night on the ice:

> The first night on the ice had been torture. The second was nightmare. Men lost their reason, began seeing visions, hearing voices. Some sank into mindless torpor, others went raving mad before death.

More men died overnight. Some simply went to sleep and never woke up, but others froze to death in a standing position while trying to keep moving during the night. As the sun began to rise, it was again impossible to tell how many men were dead. It was the morning of 2 April, and the survivors had to use the last of their strength to push forward in a final bid for the remaining men to reach safety.

Rescue and Return to St John's

The *Newfoundland* had managed to move closer to the *Bellaventure* and *Stepahno* before again becoming trapped in the ice. On the morning of 2 April, Westbury Kean was still half-convinced that his men were safely on board the *Stepahno*, and was keen to make contact with his father's ship to make sure this was the case. He was scanning the ice with his telescope when he saw small, ragged figures making their way across the ice toward him. With horror, he realised that they were the men he had put down on the ice fifty-three hours ago.

The alarm was raised and rescue parties were assembled and left the *Bellaventure*, *Stephano* and several other ships to meet the *Newfoundland* men, while the *Florizel* was contacted by radio and told to immediately make its way to the area. The *Newfoundland* men were taken on board the ships, some having to be put onto stretchers and winched on board with the crane that was usually used to load the piles of seal pelts onto the deck, as their bodies were too frozen and damaged to be taken on board any other way. The men who were still able to walk were taken to the bunks, wrapped in blankets and given hot tea, but many of those rescued from the ice were on the verge of death and drifted in and out of consciousness. Others, suffering from frozen limbs with skin that had turned black, screamed out in agony as they were brought on board.

In St John's, all of the ports, harbours and bays where the *Southern Cross* could possibly have sought shelter had been contacted, and the vessel could not be located. Ships which were out at sea, such as the revenue cutter *Seneca*, were radioed and ordered to search for the *Southern Cross*. The *Seneca* remained in contact with St John's over the wireless radio but reported that it could not find any trace of the missing vessel.

News that the *Southern Cross* was missing was starting to reach St John's. With no sightings of the vessel having been made anywhere along the coast the people of St John's slowly began to realise that the Southern Cross, and its entire crew of 173 men, had been lost in the storm. But this news was only starting to spread through the town when it started to emerge that there had been another, entirely separate, disaster on the ice. People began to learn that a group of men had been stranded on the ice overnight, with initial estimates stating that between forty and fifty of the men had lost their lives and many of the survivors had suffered terrible injuries. Family members of the missing men demanded to know if their sons and husbands were among the dead, but the chaos on the ice had seen the *Newfoundland* men taken aboard several different ships, and no clear information on survivors could be radioed to the families in St John's. Across the city, the realisation that two separate disasters, both of which involved mass loss of life, had happened simultaneously, was slowly sinking in.

On board the sealing vessels a roll call was carried out. It was eventually established that sixty-nine bodies had been recovered and eight men were missing. It was believed that all of the missing men were dead, having died on the ice and become covered in snowdrifts or had fallen off the edge of the ice sheets and into the sea. The vast majority of the injured men were placed on board the *Bellaventure*, which, after asking for permission to abandon the seal hunt from its owners, broke through the ice and began the journey back to St John's at full speed. As Cassie Brown states, for the first time ever: "The plight of injured sealers had taken precedence over the seals."

On 4 April, the *Bellaventure* arrived back at St John's. Families lined the dock, desperate to know if their husbands or sons were among the dead or injured, with rumours abounding that the loss of life would be worse than the *Greenland* disaster sixteen years earlier. In *Perished*, Jenny Higgins describes the scene:

> Hundreds of anxious spectators lined the St John's waterfront as the sealing vessel *Bellaventure* steamed through the Narrows carrying sixty-nine corpses stacked on its deck. ... Many had swollen wrists and necks, or limbs blackened by frostbite; others suffered from ice blindness and wore dark glasses.

Higgins went on to say that twenty-two of the men could not walk due their injuries and had to be removed from the ship on stretchers. A further man later died at St John's, meaning that of the 132 men who left the *Newfoundland* to go onto the ice, seventy-eight had died. Of the survivors, eleven were later classified as being permanently incapacitated due to losing limbs due to frostbite and many others were classed as partially incapacitated through the injuries they had sustained.

Inquiry and Commission

An inquiry into the disaster began just days after the *Bellaventure* returned, as the Canadian government, aware of the growing outrage over the disaster, wanted to be seen to be taking immediate action. Headed by Magistrate Arthur Knight, the inquiry called on Westbury Kean, George Tuff and Abram Kean to give evidence.

Westbury Kean stated that when he was preparing his men to go onto the ice he told George Tuff: "You reckon on the *Stephano* for the night" – a clear instruction to spend the night on board the *Stephano* after the sealing was complete. George Tuff said that he did not hear this. He testified that he interpreted his orders as being to go to the *Stephano* and then take orders from its captain, Abram Kean. Those orders were to return to the *Newfoundland* for the night, which he attempted to do. The survivors, the public and the majority of Canadian newspapers attached little blame to either Westbury Kean or George Tuff. Instead, the responsibility for the disaster was placed squarely on Abram Kean.

But Abram Kean could not attend the early stages of the inquiry as he had not returned to St John's with the other ships. Instead, after the injured men and the dead bodies had been taken away on the *Bellaventure*, he remained on the ice, ordering his men to continue sealing. Another week passed before the *Stephano* arrived at St John's, with Abram Kean seemingly unaware of the anger and fury awaiting him. When he eventually appeared at the inquiry on 13-14 April, he adopted an indignant tone, claiming that he did everything necessary to ensure that the men from the *Newfoundland* were safe. He said that he had given the men food and drink when they arrived at the *Stephano* and allowed them to rest. He had set them down close to their ship and believed that they would have no difficulty in successfully gathering thousands of seals and then returning to their ship. He maintained that he was positive that they would have been able to find the *Newfoundland* before darkness, and it never occurred to him that they may have failed to make their way back to their own ship.

This was heavily disputed at the inquiry, with maps being produced which showed that Abram Kean could not possibly have dropped the men as close to the *Newfoundland* as he claimed. At the same time, an article in the *Montreal Daily Star* was published, in which many of the survivors placed the blame on Abram Kean. Under heavy public pressure, Bowring Brothers, the owners of the *Stepahno*, removed Abram Kean from command of the vessel.

When the inquiry was published, Judge Arthur Knight said that both George Tuff and Abram Kean "Erred in their judgement that the weather would not be bad when the *Newfoundland* men left the *Stephano*." Knight also ruled that Abram Kean committed a "grave error of judgment" by sending the men back to the *Newfoundland* and preventing them from returning to his ship that night. The decision to remove the wireless radio from the *Newfoundland* was also heavily criticised, especially as this had been done on purely economic grounds as the safety aspects of having a radio were not considered important by the company. Westbury Kean was also criticised for not ensuring his men were on board the *Stephano*, and he should have constantly sounded the steam whistle of the *Newfoundland* to help the men find the ship if he had even the slightest fear at all that they were lost on the ice. But despite the criticism and blame, Arthur Knight ruled that no one was guilty of any criminal wrongdoing over the deaths of the men.

A further, more detailed Commission of Enquiry into both the *Newfoundland* and *Southern Cross* disasters then began, led by judges Sir William Horwood and Mr Justice Emerson. While the Commission would be able to apportion blame and potentially provide the basis for legal action against anyone found responsible for the loss of 251 lives across the two disasters, it would also look at safety recommendations to prevent similar tragedies from happening again.

Legal Changes

The Commission of Enquiry was published in February 1915. Like the initial Inquiry, it found that Abram Kean, Westbury Kean and George Tuff had all committed errors of judgment, but again stopped short of holding anyone criminally responsible for the disaster. The Commission was, however, highly critical of the way in which the sealing companies operated. It stated that maximising profit was the overriding aim of the sealing companies, and in order to achieve this, costs were cut through failing to provide crews with adequate clothing and safety equipment, while constantly pressurising captains to increase seal catches to the highest level possible. The Commission stated:

> The protection of human life is the paramount consideration ...
> It should not be permitted that the lives of the crew should be
> endangered by their being placed upon the ice for the night
> miles beyond the reach of any ship.

Twenty-six of the Commission's recommendations were written into law by the Newfoundland government in 1916. All sealing had to take place during daylight hours and captains had to ensure that their men were working close enough to their ships that they could return the same day. It was made mandatory for the men on the ice to carry compasses, a way of making fire and flares so that they could signal distress. All sealing ships would need to be fitted with wireless radio equipment, and the thermometers and barometers would have to be upgraded so accurate predictions of the weather conditions could be made. All sealing ships would be required to have a qualified doctor and navigator on board, and the sealing companies were made responsible for ensuring that everything possible was done to ensure the safety of the men they employed, with compensation needing to be paid to the families of sealers who lost their lives due to the negligence of the company which employed them.

The Commission also ruled on the *Southern Cross*, but with no survivors or witnesses, it could only be speculated as to what caused the loss of the vessel. It was believed that the *Southern Cross* was lost on 31 March, two miles off the coast of Newfoundland when the sea conditions, heavy rain and snowstorm of that day overwhelmed the ship. It was claimed that the *Southern Cross* may have been overloaded with seal pelts, making it unstable and that the parts of the wooden structure of the ship were rotten, possibly causing a catastrophic failure of the vessel. Furthermore, Captain George Clarke may have been taking unnecessary risks by staying out at sea in the storm in an attempt to be the first sealing ship back to St John's, instead of taking the more cautious action of sailing to the nearest port or bay to seek shelter from the weather.

The Commission criticised the lack of a wireless radio in the *Southern Cross*, again stating that, like in the *Newfoundland*, this was a cost-cutting measure that put the lives of the crew at risk. The Commission said that "better precautionary measures" needed to be put in place to stop a repeat of the disaster. Due to the belief that the *Southern Cross* may have been overloaded, they limited the number of seal pelts any vessel could return to shore with to 35,000 and also implemented an inspection system where vessels would need to be issued with a certificate which verified their seaworthiness before they were permitted to go to sea.

Following Events

The heavy criticism of Abram Kean from the Newfoundland public and press continued following the disaster. Bowring Brothers said that he would not captain the *Stephano* again and a petition calling for him to be arrested was signed by thousands of Newfoundlanders. But Abram Kean was soon back on the ice in command of the *Florizel*, although many men said they would not work under him and a public protest took place the first time he returned to the harbour at St John's to go back to sea. Despite this he continued his sealing career, captaining numerous other sealing ships. In 1934 he landed his millionth seal pelt and was awarded an OBE. In his autobiography *Old and Young Ahead!*, published in 1935, he remained defiant and continued to claim he had done nothing to contribute to the disaster of 1914. Abram Kean continued to play an active role in public life. He was appointed to the Legislative Council of Newfoundland in 1927 and was appointed as the president of the Newfoundland Board of Trade in 1928. His final season on the ice was in 1936 when he was 80 years old. He died in St John's in 1945 aged 89.

Following the disaster, Westbury Kean struggled to resume his sealing career and did not captain another ship until 1921. He then moved to

Halifax, Nova Scotia where he took a job with the company Imperial Oil. He spent his later years living in New York and was one of the last of the steam-era sealing captains when he died aged 87 in 1974.

Joseph Kean had been praised in the Commission of Enquiry for his "commendable attitude" as he was one of the first to realise that the *Newfoundland* men may be lost on the ice and tried to raise the alarm by radioing other vessels. This counted for little with Bowring Brothers, and they soon removed him from his role as captain of the *Florizel* to allow his father to take command of the vessel and resume his sealing career. Joseph Kean died when he was on board the *Florizel*, not as a crewmember but as a passenger, when it was wrecked off rocks on the southern coast of Newfoundland in 1918.

George Tuff reportedly gave up sealing a few years after the *Newfoundland* disaster. He continued to live in Newfoundland and died at the age of 56 in 1937.

The Fate of the Sealing Ships

Shortly after the disaster, the *Newfoundland* was renamed the *Samuel Blandford* and was used as a cargo vessel. It was lost when it struck rocks off St Mary's Bay off the south coast of Newfoundland in 1916 while carrying a cargo of coal from New York to St John's.

With Newfoundland being a British dominion, it became involved in the First World War when Britain declared war on Germany in August 1914. The *Stephano* was put into service as a troop carrier in 1915 and used to transport soldiers to and from various ports along the Atlantic coast of North America. It was one of the five ships which were torpedoed and sunk by the German submarine *U-53* on 8 October 1916.

The *Florizel* was also put into service as a troop carrier during the First World War and was used to take men and cargo across the Atlantic. Toward the end of the war, it was used as a passenger ship and was wrecked when it struck rocks off the coast of southern Newfoundland in February 1918 on a journey to New York via Nova Scotia. The captain at the time, William Martin, mistook the rocks, which were covered in white foam and spray, for ice, and proceeded into them at full speed. But it would later emerge that he had deliberately been given incorrect navigational information by his chief engineer who was trying to delay the journey so the *Florizel* would have to stop overnight in Nova Scotia so he could visit family. Captain Martin, therefore, believed he was much further out to sea and many miles clear of rocks and was cleared of all wrongdoing. Ninety-four people died in the disaster, including, as mentioned above, Joseph Kean, a former captain of the ship, and John Shannon Munn, a director of Bowring Brothers, the company which owned both the *Florizel* and the *Stephano*.

The *Bellaventure* was taken out of service as a Newfoundland sealing ship and sold to the Soviet Union, along with its sister ship *Bonaventure*, in 1919, and based at the port city of Archangel. Renamed the *Alexander Sibiriakov*, it was used as an icebreaker and cargo ship in the Arctic Ocean, until 1941 when it was converted into a warship. In 1942, the *Alexander Sibiriakov* became involved in a battle with the vastly superior German heavy cruiser *Admiral Scheer*. Although it was heavily outgunned and eventually destroyed, the battle lasted for over an hour and prevented the *Admiral Scheer* from intercepting an Allied convoy. For this the *Alexander Sibiriakov* is remembered as a famed Soviet ship of the Second World War.

Sealing in the Twentieth Century

Sealing with steam-powered ships continued across Newfoundland until the 1930s. But the Second World War again saw many of the sealing ships requisitioned for war service, and the Newfoundland sealing industry shrank dramatically. In the 1941 and 1942 seasons, only a single sealing vessel went out onto the ice, and in 1943, for the first time in one hundred and fifty years, there was no seal hunt in Newfoundland. J.S. Colman writes that in the years immediately following the Second World War the number of sealing ships continued to decline, with the tonnage of vessels used for sealing falling from over 12,000 tons in 1914, to 2,200 in 1947. Of these only two, the *Eagle* and the *Sable Island*, were steamers. Large steam-powered vessels had become obsolete and were replaced with smaller, more efficient diesel-powered ships.

In the second half of the twentieth century, the demand for seal products declined, and the Canadian sealing industry came under the focus of environmental campaigners due to the perceived cruelty of sealing. In the 1980s the European Economic Community (EEC) banned the importation of whitecoat seal skins. This was a hammer blow to the industry and was soon followed by the Canadian government banning the hunting of whitecoats in 1987. The European Union extended this ban, prohibiting the importation of all seal products to EU countries in 2009. The Canadian government has fought to have this overturned, claiming that such a ban violated international trade regulations, but the World Trade Organisation ruled that the ban was legal in 2014, though a small exemption allowing seal products produced by indigenous Canadian people to be imported into the EU was passed in 2015.

Today the hunting of seals continues commercially in Newfoundland and elsewhere in Canada on a small scale. Animal welfare organisations such as the International Fund for Animal Welfare continue to argue that the hunting of seals is unnecessary and cruel and campaign for the practice to be banned. But proponents of the seal hunt, backed by the Canadian government, argue that modern sealing (which sees the seals shot and not clubbed) is both humane and an important part of the nation's history and culture.

Chapter 10

FV *Destination*

FV *Destination* was an American commercial fishing boat which sank in the Bering Sea in 2017. All six crewmembers lost their lives. While the *Destination* was a rugged and robust vessel which was designed to fish in harsh Alaskan waters, a later investigation uncovered that a multitude of different factors, all of which seemed relatively innocuous when taken in isolation, combined to cause the loss of the vessel.

Commercial fishing is already one of the world's most dangerous peacetime occupations and crab fishing in the Bering Sea is one of the most dangerous forms of commercial fishing. Threats to crab fishermen include being crushed by crab pots, being swept off the deck by waves, becoming entangled in lines or winches, or being lost at sea due to their ship sinking or capsizing. It has been calculated that if a fisherman works for the full crab season they have a close to 100 per cent chance of receiving some kind of injury during their time at sea. Data from the late 1990s produced by the Center for Disease Control and Prevention, the national public health agency of the United States, outlines the dangers faced by crab fishermen. While the death rate for commercial fishermen is 140 per 100,000 workers per year, for crab fishermen operating out of Alaskan ports, this increased to 356 per 100,000 workers per year (in contrast, the death rate for the average US worker is 7 deaths per 100,000 workers per year).

The Alaskan Crab Fishery

Small-scale fishing for crab in Alaskan waters began in the first decades of the twentieth century. The Japanese fishing industry, operating in the Sea of Okhotsk and the western Bering Sea, pioneered crab fishing, using tangle nets to catch crab which were then canned at shore-based factories. Much of this canned crab was then exported from Japan to America, leading American crab fishermen to devise ways of catching Alaskan crab themselves. In the years immediately following the Second World War, specialised American crab fishing vessels were developed. Using baited crab pots, instead of inefficient tangle nets which damaged the crabs, the American crab fishing industry soon grew. The speed of this expansion was greatly increased in the 1960s when freezers began to appear in American homes. Now crab vessels could make their catches, keep the crab alive in onboard holds, and then deliver live crab to on-shore processing plants where it would be processed, frozen and sent out to supermarkets around the country. With frozen crab being of much higher quality than canned crab, demand began to increase significantly. The system of baited crab pots – which in reality were large metal cages – being dropped to the seabed and then recovered several days later is still used today.

A New System

Until 2005, the Alaskan crab fishery worked on a race-to-fish system. This meant that all vessels competed against each other to catch as much crab as possible, with the only limitation being the total annual quota which was applied to the whole fleet. This encouraged risk-taking, such as going to sea in bad weather, as boats faced reduced catches if they missed any time fishing and captains and owners were prepared to risk overloading their boats with crab pots, as they had to do everything possible to maximize catches when they were at sea. The US Marine Board of Investigation found this created an "intensely competitive derby fishery" which came to be seen as both dangerous and unsustainable.

Major safety reforms were implemented from 1999, culminating in a new crab rationalization system being introduced in 2005. Instead of a fleet-wide quota, each individual boat was given its own quota based on historic catch levels. The crab rationalization system was designed to remove the "race-to-fish" mentality from the fishery. The crab fishing season was extended, giving captains more time to prepare their boats, and crews had longer rest periods between fishing expeditions and individual quotas meant that captains could spread their catches out over time, knowing that they were no longer directly competing against other crab boats. Furthermore, a quota transfer system was implemented – if it became clear that a boat would not reach its full quota for the season, it could transfer its remaining catches to another vessel, and be compensated with a higher quota for the following season. While crab fishing in Alaskan waters remained one of the most dangerous occupations in the United States, it certainly became safer once the race-to-fish system was abolished and replaced with the crab rationalization system.

FV *Destination*

The FV *Destination* operated as a commercial fishing vessel in the Bering Sea. While it was primarily used for crab fishing, it could also be used to catch cod (using pots rather than nets) or work as a fishing tender vessel, taking supplies to other fishing ships or transporting catches to shore. Constructed by J and S Marine Services of Texas in 1981, it was originally named the *Compass Rose* and was 25 metres (81 ft) long and featured three fish holds and a crab pot loading table. In 1993 the vessel was purchased by David Wilson who changed its name to the *Destination*. It underwent modifications which included lengthening the vessel to 30 metres (98 ft) and increasing its breadth by 1.8 metres (6 ft). Following these modifications, the *Destination* had a gross tonnage of 196 tons and was capable of carrying a maximum of 200 crab pots. At the time of its loss, it was captained by Jeff Hathaway, who had been appointed to the role in 1993.

At the start of 2017, the *Destination* had spent twenty-seven days at sea fishing for cod. It returned to Sand Point, a small city with a population of just several hundred located at the point where the Alaska Peninsula meets the Aleutian Island chain, 575 nautical miles (660 miles/1,060 km) from Anchorage. Despite its small size, Sand Point is a major commercial fishing port and home to several fish and crab processing companies.

Even though they had been at sea for almost a month, the crew of the Destination would get little time on shore. As soon as the *Destination* moored at Sand Point the cod fishing gear was removed and the ship was reconfigured for crab fishing. The deck was stacked with crab pots and 15,000 gallons of diesel were taken on board, along with several barrels of engine oil and hydraulic fluid as the ship was readied to go back out to sea to catch opilio crab (also known as snow crab). But there were complications. Typically, the *Destination* would head out into the Bering Sea with relatively little bait on board. This was because it could replenish its bait supplies from a Trident Seafoods facility located on St Paul Island in the middle of the Bering Sea as and when needed. However, David Wilson, the owner of the *Destination* had been informed that Trident Seafoods had major problems procuring bait, and there were no guarantees that they could provide the required amount needed for the *Destination*. Wilson therefore contacted Hathaway and told him to "bring more bait" with him. This led to Hathaway having to take a long and convoluted journey between different harbours to collect multiple pallets of bait before he could start fishing. It also meant that the *Destination* went to sea carrying a significantly heavier load of bait than usual.

The First Stages Before the Journey to St Paul

On 8 February 2017, the *Destination* departed Sand Point and headed southwest along the Aleutian Island chain toward King Cove, a journey which took approximately nine hours. Around 4,535 kilograms (10,000 lbs) of bait was already loaded on board (the usual amount they would go to sea with) but with the news from Trident Seafoods on St Paul, they needed to take on more. On reaching King Cove they stopped at Peter Pan Seafoods where they loaded an additional 1,397 kilograms (3,080 lbs) of sardine bait on board. They then, as regulations demanded, had the *Destination* inspected by the Alaska Department of Fish and Game. The inspection was passed successfully with no issues recorded.

The *Destination* departed King Cove for Dutch Harbor, arriving at 6.30 pm on the 9 February. Jeff Hathaway contacted the Coast Guard and gave notice that he would depart in 24 hours – this was a requirement under Alaskan commercial fishing regulations. A Coast Guard petty officer then contacted Hathaway and asked if he would like a Stability and Safety Compliance Check (SSC) to be carried out on the *Destination*. This was a spot check where the vessel in question would be examined to check that it was not overloaded. Hathaway declined to have an SSC carried out, stating that if it was not a mandatory requirement he did not want the procedure carried out. At Dutch Harbor, more bait was taken on board – four pallets of squid weighing 3,202 kilograms (7,060 lbs). These pallets were loaded on top of the empty crab pots which were already on the deck.

With time to spare due to the 24-hour departure notice, Hathaway arranged for repairs to be carried out to the exhaust system of the ship and then took the crew for a meal at a nearby restaurant. Two former crewmembers of the *Destination* were also at Dutch Harbor, working on another fishing vessel which was docked there. They joined the crew for the meal, which Hathaway paid for, and the group returned to Dutch Harbor at 11.00 pm. The Marine Board of Investigation would later interview the two former crewmembers. They asked how the crew of the *Destination* appeared during the meal, having just completed a twenty-seven-day cod fishing expedition only to head back out for several more weeks to fish for crab with practically no rest time between the two trips. The former crewmembers said that the *Destination*'s crew looked "haggard" and "beat down" following the cod season, and in the restaurant, he was looking at "a table of long faces."

Freezing Spray

At Dutch Harbor, the *Destination* was low in the waterline due to the weight of the 200 crab pots, fuel and extra bait it was carrying. Indeed, when it was sailing into Dutch Harbor. Ricky Allen Fehst, the captain of another crab vessel, the *April Lane*, had asked a deckhand to take a video of the *Destination* on his mobile phone as he was concerned at how overloaded it looked. In the Coast Guard Formal Hearing into the disaster (which was held in the summer of 2017) Fehst said he was:

> Alarmed when I saw this configuration of the load that he [was] carrying ... with the forecast that we were getting northeast. The temperature was forecast to drop. And it did. ... I just said to myself, I hope they are not planning on leaving tonight with that load.

Due to the belief that the *Destination* would not be leaving the sheltered waters of Dutch Harbor loaded in that condition, he did not contact anyone on board to express his concerns. Fehst would also say that it was deemed unacceptable within the culture of Alaskan crab fishermen to contact another captain and offer unsolicited advice on the way they were running their boat. The crew of another fishing boat, the *Ocean Rover*, also took photographs of the *Destination*, as the crew were surprised by the high number of crab pots stacked on the vessel.

Fehst was particularly concerned due to the threat that freezing spray would pose to the *Destination* once it was at sea. Freezing spray occurred when the air temperature was below zero and wind conditions caused water droplets to be whipped up off the surface of the sea. When these water droplets made contact with the exposed metal of a ship they would instantly turn into ice and could soon cover the deck, rails, hull and masts of a ship. In the worst conditions, ice accumulation could be extremely rapid, with several inches of ice building up across the superstructure of the ship every hour. Crab pots were particularly susceptible to ice build-up, with their shape meaning they could not just be covered with ice, but become filled with ice. A 317 kilogram (700 lb) crab pot could increase to 907 kilograms (2,000 lb) in severe freezing spray conditions, with some crews referring to the crab pots as the 'ice cube tray' on their ship. The ice build-up caused by the freezing spray was extremely dangerous as it had the effect of raising the centre of gravity of the vessel and making it much more vulnerable to capsizing. Indeed, if left unchecked the amount of ice generated by freezing spray could add tens of tons to the weight of a ship, all of which accumulated above the waterline.

In the days leading up to the loss of the *Destination*, the US National Weather Service had issued warnings to fishing boats that conditions were such that freezing spray was a serious threat. Captains and crews were urged to take action to mitigate its impact on the stability of their ships. There were several ways in which this could be done. Some captains would delay departure until the conditions which caused freezing spray had subsided, whereas others would only operate in areas where they were protected from freezing spray, such as sheltered inshore waters. If vessels did continue to operate where they were exposed to freezing spray, crewmembers would need to climb onto the superstructure of the vessel and use rubber hammers to physically knock the ice off the ship. In conditions where freezing spray was accumulating rapidly this would need to be carried out on a regular basis. Many fishing boats operating in the same area as the *Destination* experienced severe freezing spray. The captain of the *Aleutian Lady* said that he had to break off from fishing several times so his crew could deal with freezing spray, while the captain of the *Clipper Suprise* said that freezing spray caused four inches of ice to accumulate on his ship and he was forced to abandon his usual fishing grounds and move to the sheltered waters of St George Island, next to St Paul Island, to prevent excessive amounts of ice from destabilizing his ship.

The Final Voyage

At 11.15 pm the *Destination* departed Dutch Harbor, heading approximately 232 nautical miles (266 miles/430 km) to its last stop at St Paul. Fishing would not begin with the large amount of bait on board. Instead, six pallets would be unloaded and stored at Trident Seafoods at St Paul. The *Destination* would then sail into the Bering Sea and finally begin fishing, returning to St Paul to collect the bait when it was needed.

They were set to be at sea for most of 10 February and arrive at St Paul the following day. During the journey, Hathaway spoke to other crab boat captains over the radio, discussing the best place to set their crab pots and complaining about the lack of bait available. Like the *Destination*, most other fishing vessels operating in the area had been forced to carry more bait than usual. Hathaway also made a satellite telephone call to the manager of Trident Seafoods and finalised the arrangements for the six pallets of bait to be unloaded and stored until they were needed.

At 6.13 am on 11 February, the *Destination*'s emergency position-indicating radio beacon (EPIRB) transmitted a distress alert which was picked up by the US Coast Guard's District 17 Command Center. No mayday call was issued the *Destination* did not attempt to contact any other fishing vessels by radio. A large-scale search and rescue operation was immediately launched. Nearby fishing vessels were contacted and broke away from fishing to head to the last known location of the *Destination*, and within an hour a Coast Guard HC-130 (a search and rescue version of the Lockheed C-130 Hercules military transport aircraft) was launched from Air Station Kodiak, soon followed by two Coast Guard H-60 helicopters.

The fishing vessel *Silver Spray* arrived at the last known location of the *Destination* at approximately 9.30 am and found debris and oil on the surface. One of the helicopters then located the *Destination*'s EPIRB along with crab pot marker buoys and a life ring floating on the surface and directed the *Silver Spray* to go and collect them. Searches from the air and sea continued for the rest of 11 February, and the Coast Guard cutter *Morgenthau* arrived the next day and took control of coordinating the rescue operation. If the crew had been able to don their survival suits and escape in the life raft they would very likely still be alive, and even if they were in the water wearing their survival suits they could survive for up to ten hours. However, with no mayday call being issued, it was likely that the *Destination* sank rapidly and there was very little chance that the crew had been able to prepare themselves for survival at sea. At 5.00 pm on 14 February, with more than 19,400 square kilometres (5,700 sq. miles) having been searched, the decision was made to end the rescue efforts.

Investigation and Discovery of the Wreck and Safety Alert

The Coast Guard's Marine Board of Investigation (MBI) soon began an official investigation into the incident, beginning with an analysis of the *Destination*'s Automatic Identification System (AIS), the tracking system which monitors the position and movement of ships. It was shown that the *Destination* made slow progress when travelling from Dutch Harbor to St Paul, moving at an average speed of 6.5 knots (7.5 mph), but sometimes slowing to just 1.5 knots (1.75 mph). The AIS data also showed that on two occasions on 10 February (the day before it sank) the *Destination* 'jogged' – slowed down in a low gear in order to stay in the same location and not move forward. The first jog was at approximately 1.30 pm and lasted for ten minutes, the second was between 10.00 and 11.00 pm and lasted for approximately forty minutes. The AIS data showed that, at 6.10 am, when the *Destination* had just passed St George Island, its speed reduced rapidly to less than 1 knot (1.1 mph). It maintained a forward course, but made erratic changes to its direction, before disappearing from the AIS system and soon after the EPIRB beacon activated.

In May 2017, the National Oceanic and Atmospheric Administration (NOAA) assisted the MBI in searching for the wreck of the *Destination*, with the oceanographic research vessel the *Oscar Dyson* building up a picture of the seabed using its multi-beam echo sounder. Another NOAA oceanographic research ship, the *Fairweather*, then worked from this seabed mapping and located a new wreck seven miles north of St George Island at a depth of 78 metres (256 ft). This was soon confirmed to be the *Destination*. Later that month the Coast Guard icebreaker USCGC *Healy* was able to lower a Remotely Operated Vehicle (ROV) to analyse the wreck, although only limited data could be gathered as it was difficult to operate the ROV in the harsh conditions. Two months later another ROV managed to gain further footage of *Destination*, and during this operation, the *Healy* was also able to recover a crab pot from the wreck. Due to the location of the *Destination,* it was not possible to recover the vessel. The bodies of the six crewmembers have never been found.

Following the discovery and survey of the wreck, the MBI continued their detailed investigation. Former crewmembers of the *Destination* were interviewed, along with staff at seafood facilities and ports, fishermen from other crab boats, Coast Guard staff and other officials. The MBI analysed photographs, CCTV footage, and records held by seafood facilities and ports and studied the entire history of the *Destination* to slowly build up an accurate picture of what caused the loss of the vessel. By early 2019, the official MBI report was ready for publication.

Safety Equipment and Crew

The *Destination* was carrying all of the safety and communication equipment on board which was required by law, although it was noted that the EPIRB deployed was a non-GPS model. Models equipped with GPS can transmit an accurate location as soon as they are deployed, but non-GPS models are dependent on the number of receiving satellites overhead, with the location they transmit becoming more accurate over time as they connect to more satellites. The MBI noted that there was no legal requirement for fishing vessels to be fitted with a GPS-equipped EPIRB.

The crew of the *Destination* were very experienced. Jeff Hathaway had been in command of the ship for twenty-four years. The two longest-serving deckhands both had more than twenty years on board. Two others had worked on the ship for seven years each, and the least experienced crewmember for three years. However, in their investigation, the MBI found that Hathaway's Coast Guard Merchant Mariner Credential, the general qualification held by qualified US mariners, expired in 2015, and only one deckhand had a valid Merchant Mariner Credential. As the *Destination* had a gross tonnage of 196 tons, the crew were technically not required by law to hold the qualification, as it was only mandatory for the crews of vessels with a tonnage of 200 or greater, although most owners required their crews to have such qualifications, even if it was not legally required.

Vessel Modifications, Freeing Ports and Number 3 Hatch

The owner of the *Destination*, David Wilson, grew up in Sand Point and had been associated with the Alaskan fishing industry since he was a child, buying his first fishing boat in 1977. He went to sea himself and bought the *Destination* (then named the *Compass Rose*) in 1985. In 1993 Wilson stopped going fishing to take up a role in fishing boat management, overseeing the operation of a number of other vessels in addition to the *Destination*. When the MBI looked into the work that was carried out to lengthen and widen the *Destination*, they found that no formal plans had been made by the owner or shipyard when the modifications were carried out in 1993. Instead, after the modifications were complete a naval architect had to retrospectively produce technical drawings of the *Destination* and work from these to calculate the maximum load which could be carried while maintaining stability. It was determined that a maximum of 200 standard-size crab pots could safely be carried. These were 2 metres (6.5 ft) by 2 metres by 86 centimetres (34 ins) and weighed 317 kilograms (700 lbs) when loaded with bait and gear. Following this a letter of stability was issued confirming that the newly modified *Destination* was safe to operate.

The MBI also found that the freeing ports of the *Destination* – the gaps in the bulwark which allow water to flow off the deck – did not meet regulations as they were too small. The nine freeing ports on each side of the ship covered a total area of 2,743 square centimetres (1,080 sq. ins), but a ship of the *Destination*'s size should have freeing ports which covered 6,070 square centimetres (2,390 sq. ins). This meant the freeing ports were just 54 per cent of the size they should have been, meaning that excess water would be trapped on the deck for longer than necessary. Not only would this add weight to the vessel, it would also further reduce stability as it flowed from side to side. As freeing ports were not included on the list of items to check during dockside inspections, the insufficient size of the *Destination*'s freeing ports was never discovered.

MBI analysis also unveiled another factor which could have contributed to the loss of the *Destination*. The vessel had three hatches on the deck. Once crabs were caught they would be dropped through these hatches into storage tanks in the hold. While hatch 1 and 2 were kept closed unless in use, previous crewmembers reported that Hathaway insisted that the hatch to the number 3 hold was kept open at all times, even when the *Destination* was in transit. A former crewmember told the MBI when he was on board the *Destination* he was told that hatch number 3 was always left open by order of the captain. Another former *Destination* crewmember said "Tank 3, we usually left the hatch off. Actually, we always left the hatch off." Based on this, the MBI concluded that the hatch cover was left off during the *Destination*'s journey from Dutch Harbor. This would have caused significant downflooding of number 3 hold as water splashed onto the deck. This would have reduced stability and the free surface effect – the flow of water from one side to another when the vessel was hit by waves – would have worked to prevent the *Destination* from righting itself once it started to capsize. The reason why the cover of hatch number 3 was always left open remains unknown.

Heavier Crab Pots, Additional Bait and Ice Accumulation

Another major factor in the capsizing of the *Destination* which the MBI identified was the number and type of crab pots on board. The stability instructions issued after the *Destination*'s modifications stated that up to 200 crab pots could be safely carried on the deck. This was based on each pot being the standard 2 metres by 2 metres by 86 centimetres in size and weighing 317 kilograms. However, when the crab pot which had been recovered by the *Healy* was analysed it was found to be larger at 2.1 metres (7 ft) by 2.1 metres by 86 centimetres (34 ins) and weighed 381 kilograms (840 lbs). When the MBI questioned David Wilson, it was found that he had purchased new, larger crab pots to replace the standard ones. Despite the new crab pots being substantially larger than those they replaced, the stability calculations of the *Destination* were not updated to take the new, heavier crab pots into account. With each crab pot being 63.5 kilograms (140 lbs) heavier than the one it replaced, this added another 12,700 kilograms (28,000 lbs) to the weight of the *Destination*.

Further weight was added by the additional bait that needed to be carried due to *Destination* not being able to resupply at Trident Seafoods on St Paul Island. Not only were thousands of additional pounds of bait being carried but the four pallets of squid which were taken on board at Dutch Harbor weighed 3,202 kilograms (7,060 lbs) and were placed on top of the crab pots, further raising the ship's centre of gravity and reducing its ability to maintain stability in the rough conditions.

The MBI report also believed that it was highly likely that Hathaway failed to properly deal with the ice accumulation caused by the freezing spray. He did not attempt to mitigate the impact of the freezing spray by seeking shelter or delaying departure until conditions improved. Instead, Hathaway continued directly to St Paul's, meaning it was inevitable that freezing spray would accumulate on the vessel. It appears that the only action taken was when the *Destination* 'jogged' on its way to St Paul. The ten-minute and forty-minute jogs were likely used to allow the crew to remove ice using hammers. As the MBI report noted, the jogs were of a short duration meaning that little time would have been spent removing ice and due to the exhausted condition of the crew it was highly likely that they failed to remove enough ice to improve the vessel's stability in any meaningful way.

The MBI commissioned researchers from Newfoundland Memorial University in Canada to calculate the total amount of ice which the *Destination* accumulated through freezing spray. It was found that, in a worst-case scenario, the *Destination* would have accumulated ice 30 centimetres (12 ins) thick across the ship. This would have added 96,920 kilograms (213,673 lb) of weight to the *Destination* – the equivalent of adding another 305 crab pots to the deck.

The fatigued state of the crew was seen as another contributing factor by the MBI. By fishing for cod for almost a month and then only spending a few days (which were mostly used to refit the vessel for crab fishing) the crew were exhausted and likely unable to operate at the level required for the immensely strenuous activity of commercial crab fishing in Alaskan waters. Hathaway had completely failed to take advantage of the crab rationalization system, leaving a needlessly tight timescale in which to catch their quota of crab. He also failed to ask the Trident Seafoods processing plant to push back their deadline for delivering the crab which the *Destination* caught, something the plant's owners told the MBI they would have been receptive to. Finally, under the crab rationalization system, if the *Destination* was running out of time to catch its full quota, it would have been able to transfer some of its unused quota to another boat or carry it over to the next season. This aspect of the system was specifically designed to prevent boats from having to fish intensively at the end of a season to ensure that their full quota was reached. It remains a mystery why Jeff Hathaway and David Wilson failed to do this.

Loss of FV *Destination*

With the MBI investigation complete, factors which combined to cause to loss of the *Destination* could be put together. The *Destination* arrived at Sand Point on 4 February with an exhausted and demoralised crew, having spent weeks at sea fishing for cod. Here a few days were spent on shore refuelling and refitting the vessel for crab fishing. The *Destination* then set off for King Cove where 1,360 kilograms (3,000 lbs) were added to the 4,535 kilograms (10,000 lbs) of bait that were already on board. The *Destination* then progressed to Dutch Harbor where minor repairs were carried out and four pallets of squid weighing more than 3,175 kilograms (7,000 lbs) were stacked on top of the 200 crab pots. Each crab pot was larger and heavier than those that the ship had been designed to carry, adding approximately 12,799 kilograms (28,000 lbs) to the weight of the vessel, all of which was above the waterline.

It was in this overloaded state, which the crewmembers of the *April Lane* and the *Ocean Rover* had noted, that the *Destination* left Dutch Harbor to sail to St Paul where it would drop off some of the excess bait. During this journey, the *Destination* would have been badly affected by freezing spray, which would have quickly caused ice build up on the superstructure, potentially adding many thousands of kilograms of additional weight high up on the vessel and raising the ship's centre of gravity even higher. At the same time, due to Hathaway's insistence on the hatch of hold number 3 remaining open at all times, water would have been downflooding into the hold, further reducing stability. Additional water would have been trapped on the deck, due to the insufficient size of the freeing ports. The free surface effect of the water in the hold and on the deck would also have meant that if the *Destination* did list to one side, it would be much more difficult for it to recover.

The *Destination* continued through the Bering Sea. On two occasions the *Destination* came to a stop (jogged), presumably so the crew could manually remove ice using hammers. But these were only for periods of ten and forty minutes, much too little time and the amount of ice which was removed would have led to a negligible improvement in the stability of the vessel. Forty miles from St Paul's, the *Destination* sailed along the leeward coastline of St George Island. The island would have provided some protection from the strong winds, tides and heavy waves, and once the *Destination* had passed the island it would have been exposed to the full force of the elements. The impact of these sea conditions, when combined with the excess bait on board, heavier crab pots, downflooded water and ice accumulation meant that the *Destination* could not maintain buoyancy and capsized. The crew would have had no time to launch the life raft or make a mayday call, and it was only the EPIRB emergency beacon which alerted the Coast Guard that the *Destination* had sunk.

Safety Recommendations

The MBI made a wide range of safety recommendations in their report. The Coast Guard was encouraged by the MBI to contact fishing boat owners and remind them that they were responsible for ensuring that the stability instructions regarding the maximum loads their ships could safely carry were followed. If modifications had been made, then it was the owner's responsibility to ensure that a qualified individual, such as a naval architect, carried out full and accurate updates to the ship's stability instructions.

It was also recommended that crab pots were weighed to ensure they matched the weight stated in the vessel's stability instructions. If new crab pots had been purchased, they needed to be checked to ensure that they were not heavier than those the vessel had been designed to carry. This highlighted the issue of weight creep – the process of fishing boats getting progressively heavier over time as parts were replaced, fishing gear was upgraded and new equipment was added. Furthermore, the MBI recommended that it should be a mandatory requirement for fishing boat captains to attend Coast Guard-approved courses on vessel stability.

The procedure for checking and inspecting vessels, and ensuring that Stability and Safety Compliance Checks were carried out was strengthened, with a sample of crab pots being removed from fishing boats to be weighed and checked against the stability instructions as part of these inspections. Owners would also have to record all alterations and modifications which had been made to their vessels so that the weight could be tracked over time. This would also allow the Coast Guard to check the weight of vessels against stability instructions. Further measures were also put in place so that the impact that fatigue would have on crew performance would be more closely monitored. The MBI stated that this would require crab boat owners and captains to implement a rest policy for their crews which would "give crewmembers the opportunity to reduce their risk of fatigue-related accidents and help prevent casualties."

Deadliest Catch

The loss of the *Destination* became came to the attention of an international audience after it was included in an episode of the Discovery Channel television programme *Deadliest Catch*. Although the *Destination* was not a featured boat on the programme and did not have an embedded film crew, the ship and its crew were well known to the fishermen who regularly appeared in the programme. The season thirteen episode, entitled *Lost at Sea,* was broadcast in August 2017 and showed the featured crews responding to the news that the *Destination* was missing. Several prominent fishermen in the programme, most notably Sig Hansen, the captain of the FV *Northwestern*, were seen to react with devastation at the news. After the episode was aired, donations to a fund which had been set up to raise money for the crewmembers' families increased significantly.

Chapter 11

José Salvador Alvarenga

In November 2012 two fishermen boarded a small boat and set off into the Pacific Ocean from the coast of Mexico. They were meant to be at sea for around thirty hours but would become caught in a heavy storm. One man would die, while the other would end up fighting for his life and spending an inordinately long time lost and adrift at sea.

José Salvador Alvarenga was born in the Central American country of El Salvador in the mid-1970s (there are conflicting reports on exactly when he was born). He spent his early life in the town of his birth, Garita Palmera. He had little formal education, having left school aged 11 or 12, but was always willing to carry out hard, physical work. This led him to work as a fisherman, although he had also taken other manual jobs when this was necessary. By the early 2000s, Alvarenga had a wife and a baby daughter named Fatima.

At some time in 2002 (the exact date is unclear) Alvarenga became involved in a bar fight after a heavy night of drinking in a town near his home. What exactly happened is uncertain, but reports state that he was badly beaten and stabbed and spent at least two weeks in hospital. Although he made a full recovery, Alvarenga became convinced that his assailants would come after him, and became too afraid to go out in public. This, combined with the belief that he could make more money as a fisherman outside of El Salvador, led Alvarenga to decide to leave his wife and daughter to move to Mexico. Alvarenga entered Mexico illegally via Guatemala, without the requisite work visa or immigration papers, successfully posing as a Mexican citizen to gain access to the country. Alvarenga made his way to Chiapas, Mexico's southernmost and poorest state, and settled in the coastal town of Costa Azul.

Costa Azul Fishing Community

The small fishing community at Costa Azul consisted of around one hundred fishermen and was based around a coastal lagoon, set back from the beautiful sandy beaches. With Alvarenga's experience and willingness to work hard, employment as a fisherman was easy to come by, and no questions were asked about his immigration status or lack of work documents. While the area was usually calm, this part of the Pacific Ocean was known for storms, which, while rare, could be very powerful, with the lagoon acting as a natural shelter and harbour for the fishing boats. There were no trawlers, dredgers or other large fishing vessels operating out of Costa Azul. The fishing boats the Mexican fishermen used were small, just 7 or 8 metres (23 – 26 ft) in length, with a crew of one or two, and were used to carry out longline fishing. This consisted of going out to sea and setting hundreds of baited hooks on a line suspended across the surface by floats. The line would be left, sometimes for hours and sometimes overnight, and then recovered, with species such as tuna, marlin, dolphinfish (also known as mahi-mahi) and various species of shark all being caught. While profitable catches could once be made just miles from the shore, declining fish stocks meant they had to venture further and further out to sea with most fishermen now usually travelling more than fifty miles from shore to set their lines.

While Alvarenga had a boss, who he only knew by the name of Willy, there were few laws, rules or regulations governing the fishermen of Costa Azul. All payments, typically less than a dollar per kilogram of fish caught, were made in cash and workers such as Alvarenga were free to conduct their fishing as they saw fit, making their own decisions on which area to fish, how long to stay out at sea and deciding for themselves if the weather and sea conditions were safe to go to sea. As long as the catches were made, the workers would be paid and bosses such as Willy would be happy. Despite the informal nature of their employment and the fact that each boat was effectively competing against the others for catches, the working relationships between the fishermen were close. An unwritten code existed between the men, dictating that they would help each other with everything ranging from boat and engine maintenance to rescuing fellow fishermen who ended up in trouble while out at sea.

Indeed, the culture of the fishermen, many of whom were single men who lived in small shacks near the lagoon, was one of wild partying. In the time they had free between fishing trips almost all of the men spent the money they made from fishing on heavy drinking, smoking marijuana, going to bars and chasing after women. Alvarenga also took up this lifestyle during his time in Costa Azul, making no attempt to stay in contact with his wife and daughter back in El Salvador, and failing to send any of the money he made back to them.

The Voyage

By 2012, Alvarenga, then in his mid-thirties, had been part of the Costa Azul fishing community for years, and had worked his way up to be regarded as one of its most experienced and successful fishermen. He was in command of his own boat, a 7.5 metre (25 ft) fibreglass skiff. It was powered by a Yamaha outboard motor, had no rudder (changes in direction were made by moving the motor) and was open to the elements as it did not feature any kind of cabin or roof.

Alvarenga prepared to go on what should have been a routine fishing trip. He would set off on the morning of 17 November 2012, spend the night at sea and return the following day after around thirty hours. He would not be alone. A novice fisherman named Ezequiel Córdoba would be accompanying him. Aged 22, Córdoba was relatively new to fishing and had been placed with Alvarenga to gain experience. This was common in Costa Azul, and was seen as mutually beneficial – Alvarenga would be able to fish more efficiently with an extra person on board, while Córdoba would learn the skills and techniques he would need to one day run his own boat.

The small boat was loaded with everything Alvarenga would need for the voyage out into the Pacific. This consisted of hundreds of metres of line, fitted with around 700 hooks, sardines for bait, food, extra fuel, a battery-powered radio and a handheld non-waterproof GPS. He did not take an anchor, believing that as he would be many miles from the coast and fishing in very deep water, an anchor would not reach the seabed and was therefore unnecessary. He also lacked flares to signal distress or an emergency backup motor.

As they left the sheltered lagoon and headed out into the Pacific Ocean the sea began to turn choppy and dark clouds formed overhead. Alvarenga was not particularly concerned, having dealt with harsh conditions many times before in his fishing career. Once they reached the fishing grounds the hooks were baited and dropped over the side of the boat, ready to be recovered the following day. But as they continued to bait and set hooks the weather continued to worsen. The size of the waves increased and Córdoba became increasingly frightened by the conditions and asked to go back to shore. Alvarenga initially refused, wanting to continue fishing but soon changed his mind and agreed that they should head back. They began to recover the longline, and although it had not been in the sea for anywhere near as long as planned, many fish were already hooked, meaning that even though they were cutting short their time at sea, it had not been a wasted journey. But as they continued the laborious process of hauling the line on board, unhooking fish and placing them in the large icebox fitted to the boat, conditions rapidly grew worse. Alvarenga made the decision to sever the longline and head back immediately. While abandoning the longline (and the valuable fish which would be hooked on it) at sea was far from ideal, the changing conditions left him with no choice.

The journey back became increasingly difficult. Their boat was battered by the waves which had increased to 3 - 4 metres (9 - 12 ft) in height, sheets of rain came down and the wind continued to increase in power, whipping up the surface of the sea into a white foam. The small boat was tossed around, but still made steady, if slow progress, heading back toward Costa Azul and the safety of the lagoon, although the splashing waves and heavy rainfall were beginning to fill the boat with water, and Alvarenga instructed Córdoba to bail out the water with a bucket. Eventually, the handheld GPS, now covered in water, stopped working, but Alvarenga was not overly concerned as he could see land through the rain and spray and was confident he could navigate back to the lagoon without the GPS.

But when they were around twenty miles from land the Yamaha motor spluttered and then gave out. Alvarenga tried to restart it but it was no use, no matter what he tried, the motor remained dead. Using the radio, Alvarenga contacted his boss on shore and explained that he was in an emergency situation. His boss asked for his GPS coordinates, but with the unit soaking wet and not functioning, Alvarenga was unable to supply them. He was then instructed to lower the anchor and wait until a fishing boat could be readied to come and rescue them, but Alvarenga had to explain that his boat was not equipped with an anchor. His boss told him that they would try and send a boat to come and assist them, but they may need to wait for the storm to subside before this could be done. Shortly after this conversation the batteries of the radio, which had only been half charged when they set off, died.

Lost at Sea

With no means of communication or propulsion, Alvarenga and Córdoba were at the mercy of the elements. Waves continued to smash over the boat, sending equipment crashing over the deck and into the sea and both men had to hold on to anything they could to avoid being tipped out of the boat. When conditions calmed slightly, it became clear that through the rainfall and waves, the boat was taking on water to such an extent that it would sink, so both men furiously bailed water with buckets until the boat stabilized. Alvarenga gave the order for anything unnecessary to be thrown into the sea to lighten the boat, and any remaining equipment, as well as the fish they had caught and the ice they were stored in, were dropped overboard. Eventually, although the storm still raged, the boat stabilized and Alvarenga realised that, as long as they kept bailing out water, they would not capsize or sink.

When the storm eventually subsided, days had passed, but through Alvarenga's quick thinking, and the physical effort of constantly bailing out water, they had survived. Alvarenga and Córdoba hoped that the other fishermen would now, in the calmer conditions, be able to send a boat out to locate and rescue them, but they had no idea that the storm had taken them almost 480 kilometres (300 miles) out to sea. While their fellow fishermen had sent out multiple boats to look for them, and even managed to employ the services of a light aircraft to search for them, they were already far beyond the range of these search efforts. They were lost at sea, on their small boat, with no motor, sails or oars, no food, no equipment and no means of signalling for help.

Alvarenga and Córdoba had no other choice than to switch into survival mode. They scooped jellyfish from the sea to eat and drank their own urine to try and stay hydrated. The blazing sun soon started to burn their skin and they had to both clamber into the large icebox, which had been used to store the fish they caught, to shelter from the sun. The space was so small and confined that the two men had to squeeze together to fit inside, but, during the hottest hours of the day when the sun was directly overhead, they had little other option.

By the end of the first week, they were around 800 kilometres (500 miles) from the coast of Mexico and continuing to drift eastwards, further and further into the Pacific Ocean. With both men almost starving, Alvarenga made a discovery. Many turtles came to their boat to shelter underneath it, and Alvarenga found that he could catch the turtles by hand. The meat could be eaten and they could drink the creature's blood. As unpalatable as this may seem, it kept them alive. Still, obtaining fresh water became a priority, with Alvarenga and Córdoba cutting open the plastic bottles and placing them around the boat, ready to collect rainwater. After two weeks of drinking urine and turtle blood and licking the early morning dew from the deck of the boat, it eventually rained, giving the men a supply of water which they would ration so it would last for weeks.

Further into the Pacific

Further weeks passed and the men managed to catch the small fish which came to their boat, and, as they got further and further out into the Pacific Ocean, seabirds came down to their boat to rest. Alvarenga learned to catch these birds, keeping them alive by tethering them to the boat with the small length of rope they had and creating a new food source. While they had no means of starting a fire, the fish, turtle and bird meat could be left out in the sun to dry, making it more palatable than being eaten raw. A further source of food came with the small sharks which began to swim alongside their boat. Alvarenga was sometimes able to catch these sharks, although the rough skin tore into his hands as he pulled them from the water and they would squirm and spin and try to bite him. But once the sharks were on the boat and killed their flesh and nutrient-filled liver provided another vital source of food for the two men.

By the time 2012 turned to 2013, they had drifted several thousand miles out into the Pacific. While they now had a semi-regular food supply, Córdoba grew increasingly despondent, believing they would never be found. Alvarenga continued to eat all of the sea creatures they could catch, but Córdoba began to eat less and less. Deeply religious, he claimed that drinking turtle blood was a sin and that he could become poisoned by eating anything other than fish. He grew weaker and weaker, and Alvarenga soon realised that his shipmate was dying. He placed Córdoba in the icebox and promised that, if he survived, he would visit Córdoba's mother and pass on his last words to her. A few days later, Córdoba peacefully died while resting in the icebox. Unsure of what to do with the body, Alvarenga left it onboard and continued to talk to Córdoba as if he was still alive. But the sun soon turned Córdoba's skeletal corpse black. Alvarenga became worried that talking to a dead body would eventually send him insane and made the decision to place Córdoba's body into the sea and watched as it sank out of sight.

Alvarenga Alone

Now alone, Alvarenga redoubled his effort to survive. He was becoming increasingly efficient at catching fish and seabirds, and when it did rain he was able to conserve enough water to last him until it rained again. Thousands of miles away from the nearest landmass, Alvarenga continued this way of life for months. His clothes slowly disintegrated, his skin became increasingly sunburned, and his face became covered in a bushy beard. In his book on Alvarenga's ordeal, the writer and journalist Jonathan Franklin explains that, as he spent day after day at sea, Alvarenga came to reflect on his life. He regretted walking out on his family and felt ashamed that he would not recognize his daughter if he saw her now. He promised that if he did survive he would change his ways and give up drinking, marijuana and partying, and dedicate himself to his daughter and family.

The days and months continued to pass, and Alvarenga eventually drifted into the Intertropical Convergence Zone, better known as the Doldrums. Here, there was almost no wind or currents, and the speed at which the boat was drifting across the Pacific slowed and slowed until it was hardly moving at all. Alvarenga had no idea how long he had been at sea, only knowing that through his observations of the moon, it had been many, many months. Occasionally he would see cargo ships, sometimes in the distance, sometimes relatively near. But his boat was tiny in comparison to such vessels and sat low in the water with no mast. It would take a miracle for someone on board to see him and his boat, and as much as he waved and shouted when he saw a ship, he was never spotted by anyone.

Unsure of how long he had been at sea, only knowing it was a very, very long time, Alvarenga began to lose hope. His body was breaking down, he was becoming weaker and he was finding it harder and harder to hunt fish and catch seabirds. Jonathan Franklin describes how Alvarenga thought that a cargo ship passed right by him, and he even saw several men fishing with rod and line, who waved to him from the back of the ship. Believing he was rescued Alvarenga began to celebrate, but the men did not attempt to stop their vessel or send a small boat to come and assist him. Devastated, Alvarenga returned to the icebox to rest. Confused and angry, he slowly came to realize that the cargo ship had, in all likelihood, never existed, and had been a hallucination conjured up by his increasingly confused mind.

Land at Last

Then, one night, Alvarenga saw lights on the distant horizon. Unable to exactly identify what they were, Alvarenga thought that they may be cargo vessels, trawlers or some other type of ship. He continued to drift toward them, and, as he grew nearer and nearer he realised that he had finally reached land. As his boat reached shallow water, he jumped out into the sea, and made his way through the water and onto the beach, finally placing his feet on dry land. Overwhelmed, and unsure if he was hallucinating again, Alvarenga crawled along the beach, and then, exhausted fell asleep. It was 30 January 2014 – he had been adrift on the Pacific Ocean for 438 days.

Alvarenga had drifted over 6,000 miles from the coast of Mexico to Ebon Atoll, a small island chain on the edge of the Republic of the Marshall Islands, one of the most remote places on Earth. Ebon Atoll only had a population of around 700, a single telephone line, and the larger settlements of the Marshall Islands could only be reached by boat. Although he didn't know it, Alvarenga had set a world record, being the first person in history to survive for more than a year alone at sea.

When he awoke, Alvarenga began searching around the island, looking for sources of food. Husband and wife Emi Libokmeto and Russell Laikidrik lived in a small house near to the beach on Ebon Atoll where they made a living harvesting coconuts. Libokmeto told the *Guardian* that as she was working "I see this white man there ... He is yelling. He looks weak and hungry. My first thought was, this person swam here, he must have fallen off a ship." Libokmeto and Laikidrik went out to meet Alvarenga. He was weak and confused, wearing only shredded scraps of clothes. They were unable to speak with him as neither spoke Spanish, but, communicating with hand gestures, they were able to convince him to come into their home. There they were able to care for him and make him pancakes, which he devoured. Libokmeto and Laikidrik sent for help, and soon the island's mayor was informed and a nurse and Marshall Islands officials came to Ebon Atoll to see the new arrival for themselves.

But Alvarenga was agitated and unnerved, suspicious of the people now here to see him and frightened that he may be arrested. After a while, the mayor's son, who spoke a little Spanish, arrived and acted as a translator. Now knowing that he would not be arrested and the people around him were there to help him, Alvarenga calmed down. He stayed on Ebon Atoll for a few days, receiving medical attention and being fed meals of rice and chicken. Alvarenga agreed to be transported by boat to the capital of Majuro, where he would be admitted to hospital. However, in the days since he arrived on the Marshall Islands news of Alvarenga and his almost incomprehensible journey had spread and become a major story across the world's media. When he arrived at Majuro journalists and reporters from as far away as Australia and the USA were waiting for him and photographed him as he shuffled off the boat and onto the dockside, a can of Coca-Cola in one hand. Hundreds of interview requests were made, all of which were rejected. Even in his hospital bed, Alvarenga was not safe from media attention, with a journalist reportedly posing as a doctor to gain access to his room to speak to him.

Recovery and Suspicions

While Alvarenga was in hospital in Majuro, much of the media speculation began to focus on his improbable story. Many believed that it was simply impossible for a human to survive for so long on the meagre food sources available to Alvarenga, while it was also speculated that crossing three-quarters of the Pacific Ocean in a small, unpowered boat would have taken longer than fourteen months. Marshall Island's officials added credibility to these claims with Gee Bing, the Marshall Island's Secretary of Foreign Affairs, being quoted in the *Guardian* as saying that he was "not sure if he believe[d] his story" as Alvarenga was "not really thin" leading to Bing "having some doubts." An article in the *Telegraph* at the time stated that doctors were surprised by the relatively good condition Alvarenga was in, and they expected him to be much more emaciated and in worse health after enduring such an ordeal.

Alvarenga did not help the situation with some of the responses he gave when officials were trying to verify his identity. In *438 Days: An Extraordinary True Story of Survival at Sea,* Jonathan Franklin explains that, when asked, Alvarenga spelt his name in several different ways, gave different dates of birth, did not know the name of the company he worked for and could only name his boss by the single name of 'Willy.' He also provided conflicting details of his family members in El Salvador. But as time passed and more details came to light, corroborating evidence began to emerge which strengthened Alvarenga's story. Using the serial number on the side of his boat, the Marshall Islands government was able to trace it back to Costa Azul, and Alvarenga's colleagues – amazed at the news he was alive – were able to confirm that he had gone missing during a storm fourteen months previously.

Furthermore, Alvarenga was not in as good physical condition as his initial appearance suggested. Although he was undoubtedly less thin than might be expected for someone who had undergone such an ordeal, the medics who treated him said that this was due to a condition called edema. This causes swelling when water becomes trapped in the body's tissues causing a bloated and swollen appearance. Further assessments showed that when he first landed at Ebon Atoll, the level of vitamins and minerals in Alvarenga's body were dangerously low, his blood pressure was also low and the swelling of his feet, ankles and knees made it difficult for him to walk and he was showing signs of liver damage. Alvarenga's muddled answers about his personal details, family and employment status were put down to confusion caused by his fragile mental state after fourteen months alone at sea.

Oceanographers carried out research into the route which Pacific Ocean currents took Alvarenga from the coastline of Mexico to the Marshall Islands. Dr Erik Van Sebille, an oceans scientist who was based at the University of New South Wales, said that while the expected time to drift the distance Alvarenga covered was between eighteen months and two years, it was perfectly possible for it to be completed in fourteen months. Alvarenga was fortunate to have reached the Marshall Islands. If the winds and currents had taken him slightly further north or south he would have bypassed the islands and reached the western portion of the Great Pacific Garbage Patch – a huge collection of mostly plastic marine debris hundreds of miles across which is trapped by ocean gyres in the Pacific Ocean. Here he may have become trapped in a circular ocean current and never made land, and even if he had been able to escape he would have had another 5,500 km (3,450 miles) to drift to reach the next landmass, the Philippines.

After nine days in hospital in Majuro, Alvarenga was considered healthy enough to travel back to El Salvador. His family, including his parents who he had lost contact with many years ago, had become aware of his new-found fame through the massive worldwide publicity his story had generated and stated that they looked forward to seeing him again. The journey back to El Salvador was long, taking more than thirty hours (including stopovers) and was the first time Alvarenga had ever been on an aeroplane. The first leg took Alvarenga from Majuro to Hawaii, where he spent a night in a hotel, and then flew from Hawaii to Los Angeles, and then on to El Salvador and his hometown of Garita

Palmera. In order to aid his journey US officials and medics flew with Alvarenga and he was allowed to bypass the usual customs and security checks, although there was an incident on the way to Los Angeles where two journalists, who had booked themselves on the same flight to try and interview Alvarenga had to be kept away from him by the US officials.

Return to El Salvador and Legal Issues

Back in El Salvador, Alvarenga reunited with his family and moved back into his parent's home, but did not immediately go back to his old life. He was represented by a lawyer named Benedicto Perlera, a long-term friend of the family who handled interview requests and publicity. Perlera arranged for Alvarenga to sit a lie detector test, which he passed, helping to end the lingering speculation that his story may not be true. He then flew to Mexico, where he visited the family of Ezequiel Córdoba and told his mother the story of her son's last days and assured her that he died peacefully. Alvarenga then travelled back to Costa Azul to see his colleagues in the fishing community. Jonathan Franklin writes that Alvarenga was initially hostile, believing that they had failed to search for him when he first radioed to tell them that he was in trouble, and was outraged that, after he had been missing for one year they had registered him as legally dead, in accordance with Mexican law. However, after speaking with them for some time, and realising that his colleagues had risked their own lives to go out to sea in their fishing boats to look for him when the storm was still raging and then commissioned an aircraft to continue the search, Alvarenga accepted that they had done all they could. A party was held that night, and although Alvarenga attended, he did not drink any alcohol or smoke marijuana.

But legal troubles were the next challenge that Alvarenga would have to overcome. In 2015 it was announced that Alvarenga was being sued for $1 million by the family of Córdoba, who now accused him of cannibalism, claiming that when their son died Alvarenga ate the body and threw Córdoba's corpse into the sea to hide what he had done. Alvarenga has always strongly denied any accusations of cannibalism, stating that he and Córdoba had an agreement that whoever was the first to die would not eat the other. In 2014, *Daily Mail* journalist David Jones travelled to El Salvador to interview Alvarenga. When asked if he ever considered cannibalism Alvarenga said:

> No! Never! Not for one second did I think of eating Ezequiel ... wouldn't have done it, even if it meant that I starved. It would have been on my conscience forever.

He added that when Córdoba died, the food supply on the boat was, by the standards of the journey, plentiful, consisting of birds, turtles and fish, negating the need to eat his friend.

It later emerged that as well as being sued for cannibalism, the Córdoba family were also suing Alvarenga for future earnings, as he had signed a deal to have a book on his ordeal published and they believed that they were entitled to half of the profits. The Córdoba family were represented by Benedicto Perlera, who had stopped representing Alvarenga following an argument during their visit to Mexico and switched allegiances to represent Córdoba's family. The book, the previously mentioned *438 Days: An Extraordinary True Story of Survival at Sea*, by the Chile-based American author and journalist Jonathan Franklin, was based on hours of interviews with Alvarenga, as well as survival experts, and the officials and medics who saw Alvarenga when he reached the Marshall Islands. It was released on 17 November 2015, three years to the day since Alvarenga and Córdoba set off on their fateful journey, and received positive reviews.

As of 2024, there have been no updates on the progress of the cannibalism or book deal lawsuits against Alvarenga, and as so much time has passed since they were first announced it can only be assumed that they have been dismissed, especially as the Córdoba family had no evidence to back up their cannibalism claims. Information on Alvarenga's life since his return to El Salvador is also difficult to come by. The latest verifiable information comes from Franklin's book which, states that, as he promised himself when he was at his lowest point adrift on the Pacific Ocean, Alvarenga had reconciled with his daughter and family and was living a quiet life back in El Salvador and was thinking of working as a fisherman once again.

Chapter 12

The Seaham Lifeboat Disaster

In 1962 a small fishing boat with five people on board became caught in a storm off the coast of Seaham. A lifeboat containing five crewmembers was sent out to assist, but would itself get into trouble as the weather continued to deteriorate. Of the ten people involved in the disaster, only one would survive.

Seaham is a town in County Durham in North East England. From the mid-1800s until the late twentieth century three large coal mines provided steady, although dangerous, employment for the local population and became a major component of the town's economy. The production of coal meant that Seaham Harbour, which was completed in 1828, was busy with colliers – cargo ships designed specifically to carry coal – constantly arriving and departing. The volume of shipping using the harbour led to safety improvements including a lifeboat station consisting of a boathouse and launch ramp, which was built on the harbour's north dock in the 1870s. This meant that a lifeboat was permanently on station at Seaham Harbour, ready to respond to ships in distress.

Liverpool-class lifeboats and the *George Elmy*

A number of Royal National Lifeboat Institution (RNLI) lifeboats were stationed at Seaham from 1870, and by 1936 a Liverpool-class lifeboat, the *Elizabeth Wills Allen*, was Seaham Harbour's dedicated lifeboat.

The Liverpool-class lifeboats had been developed in the early 1930s and became the main type of lifeboat used across Britain. They were constructed mostly of wood, were 10 metres long (35 ft), displaced eight tons, and were powered by a single six-cylinder engine, although they also retained a sail as a backup in case of engine failure.

The *Elizabeth Wills Allen* served as Seaham Harbour's lifeboat for fourteen years and was launched seventeen times, saving fourteen lives. But by the late 1940s, a new variation of Liverpool-class lifeboats had been developed. These were larger, with improved stability, and, as they were twin-engined, the sail could be removed. In 1950, a new Liverpool-class lifeboat, which had been constructed in Cowes on the Isle of Wight by Groves and Gutteridge, was delivered to Seaham. A legacy from Miss Elizabeth Elmy of Stoke Newington in London had funded the procurement of the lifeboat. She had no connection with Seaham or the North East of England and had provided the legacy for the RNLI to purchase a lifeboat to use anywhere in Britain, with her only stipulation being that it was named after her late brother. The *George Elmy* proved just as dependable as its predecessor, being called out twenty-six times and rescuing twenty people between 1950 and 1962.

The *Economy* and the Growing Storm

Early in the morning of Saturday, 17 November 1962, three men left Seaham Harbour on their small fishing boat, the *Economy*, a coble built in 1892. They were miners – not commercial fishermen – and were fishing for pleasure. Fishing was a hugely popular pastime for the men who worked in the mines and many would spend their days off at sea, with dozens of small fishing boats being located at Seaham. In the late morning, the *Economy* returned to Seaham Harbour, but the men made plans to go back out to sea again later in the day.

By the Saturday afternoon, the sea had become choppy and the wind picked up, but the men kept to their plan. At around 2.45 pm. the *Economy* once again left the harbour and headed toward its fishing grounds. This time there were four men on board – Joseph Kennedy, George Firth, Gordon Burrell and Donald Burrell, along with 9-year-old David Burrell, the son of Donald Burrell. The *Economy* was closely followed out of the harbour by another fishing boat, the *Silver Spray*.

Both fishing boats went their separate ways, the *Economy* heading two miles out to sea, but the *Silver Spray* stayed relatively close to the shore. However, the weather continued to worsen. The size of the waves was building, and the windspeed increased, with spray being whipped off the sea, reducing visibility. After less than an hour at sea the men on the *Silver Spray* abandoned fishing and headed back to the harbour. But as they made their way back the conditions deteriorated further. The waves continued to grow and the windspeed increased to gale force as a storm set in. While they managed to make it back to the safety of Seaham Harbour, they knew that the *Economy*, much further out to sea, would have serious difficulties in making its way back to the harbour. As soon as the men from the *Silver Spray* arrived back at Seaham they informed Captain R. Hudson, the secretary of the Seaham Lifeboat Station, that there was still a fishing boat out at sea which would require immediate assistance.

The Disaster

At 3.55 pm Captain Hudson gave the order to launch the maroons – a type of signalling rocket – to call the lifeboat crew to their station. The crew of five – led by Coxswain John Miller – soon arrived and just ten minutes later the *George Elmy* glided down the slipway and into the North Sea. Battling driving rain and wind, Miller steered the *George Elmy* out of the harbour and toward the distress flares that had been launched by the men in the *Economy*. Despite the conditions, the *George Elmy* progressed steadily through the heaving seas, closing in on the *Economy*. But the weather continued to worsen, the wind increasing to gale-force, with storm-force gusts and the waves growing in height to more than 3.5 metres (12 ft).

At around 4.30 pm the *George Elmy* reached the *Economy*, and Miller decided the best course of action was to pull alongside and take the crew on board his boat. He manoeuvred the *George Elmy* as close as he could, and made three attempts to throw a rope across to the *Economy*, but was thwarted each time by the waves and wind. On the fourth attempt Miller succeeded, and the two boats were pulled together and all five people from the *Economy* were taken onboard the *George Elmy*. Miller then contacted the harbour master by radiotelephone and informed him that they were returning. But as the *George Elmy* made its way back toward the harbour, the storm continued to intensify with the rain turning to sleet, and the strength of the wind and the size of the waves continuing to increase

The *George Elmy* came into view of Captain Hudson and others in the lifeboat station when it was several hundred metres away from the harbour. They watched it draw closer, but with the storm now in full force, and the spray, rain and waves severely reducing visibility, Miller and the crew had difficulty in locating the entrance to the harbour. Eventually, they saw the lighthouse at the end of the north pier and managed to make their way toward the harbour entrance. They were close to safety, but this was the most dangerous part of the return journey. Miller would have to turn the *George Elmy* broadside on to the wind and waves in order to enter the harbour. The distance to the harbour entrance was less than the length of the lifeboat when Miller made the manoeuvre and turned the lifeboat into position to sail between the piers. But as he did so a succession of waves struck the *George Elmy*, capsizing it and sending the ten people on board into the raging sea. The men tried desperately to cling on to the upturned lifeboat, but the force of the waves made this impossible for all but one, who managed to grip onto the propellers. The *George Elmy* was pushed and buffeted by the wind and waves toward the shore, ending up wrecked next to Liddle Stack on Chemical Beach, just a few hundred metres away from the harbour. Donald Burrell, the man who had clung to the propeller, managed to crawl onto the beach, where exhausted, he collapsed.

The Search

A search for survivors was immediately launched, with the rescue teams knowing they would have to be found quickly. The weather was freezing, and any survivors would soon die of cold and exposure even if they did make it to the beach. Donald Burrell was quickly found and taken to hospital, and with the *George Elmy* capsizing so close to the harbour it was hoped that many of the fishermen and lifeboat crew would be forced to the shoreline by the storm, and they would soon be located.

Police took control of the situation and began searches of the beach, assisted by local people who left the nearby pubs and their homes to join the search parties. Managers of the nearby Dawdon Colliery lent mining lamps and lanterns to those involved in the searches. By 7.00 pm there were around two hundred people involved in the search, covering two miles of coastline. Lifeboats from nearby Hartlepool and Sunderland were launched to search the sea, and an Avro Shackleton maritime patrol aircraft was launched from RAF Acklington in Northumberland, which dropped flares over the sea to light up the area for the lifeboats. Searchlights were set up on the clifftops too scour the beaches, but the weather and terrain of the area were against the rescuers. As James Devlin, a police officer in Seaham at the time, wrote in 1968:

> It was freezing cold, the wind was at hurricane force, whipping up the waves to a fantastic height and it was raining heavily ...
> Apart from the weather the searchers were faced with the difficult geographical position of the disaster, the area being strewn with large boulders and sea-filled holes.

A mobile police station was also set up to coordinate the rescue effort, and the fire brigade and special constables (part-time volunteer police officers) also arrived and were assigned new areas of the coastline to search. A temporary canteen was set up in the grounds of Dawdon Colliery to provide hot drinks and food to rescuers who were working overnight, and members of the Salvation Army also arrived to offer their support. The search for survivors continued all night but the following day at 4.00pm, with twenty-four hours having passed since the disaster and no survivors being found, the decision was made to call off the rescue operation.

Over the next three days the bodies of six of the men and the boy were found, washed up on beaches within twelve miles of Seaham. Another body was found the next month at Redcar, approximately 22 miles south of Seaham. The body of one of the men was never recovered.

The Inquest and Support for the Families

A coroner's inquest was held one month later in Seaham in December 1962. In an edition of *The Journal of the Royal National Life-boat Institution*, issued just months after the disaster in March 1963, it was stated that the coroner attached no blame to Miller or the crew of the *George Elmy*:

> The lifeboat was justified in setting out, the coxswain was thoroughly competent and the life-boat seaworthy, and he was confident that no blame should be attached to the coxswain for the loss of life.

Instead, the cause of the disaster was put down to the treacherous conditions of the sea and the rapidly worsening weather which the crew of the *George Elmy* had no way of predicting. The coroner asked for permission from the Home Secretary to record the death of the crewmember who had not been recovered as death by accidental drowning which was granted. A separate inquiry carried out by the RNLI reached the same conclusions.

The *George Elmy* had been inspected by a surveyor who had travelled to Seaham from London the day after the disaster. He found that there was damage to the stern and hull caused by its grounding on the beach and damage caused to the electrical components and engine due to water ingress. But all of the damage had been caused after it capsized and prior to this the *George Elmy* was a well-maintained and seaworthy lifeboat.

While the town of Seaham was in mourning, tributes to the men came in from across the country. Princess Marina, Duchess of Kent, who was the president of the RNLI at the time, sent a telegram to express her sympathy. Members of parliament discussed the disaster in the House of Commons, letters were published in national newspapers and it was revealed that the RNLI had sent a donation of £500 for the immediate needs of the families. Miller's son, who had been on a ship sailing to South Africa at the time of the disaster, was contacted by telegram, and was able to return home in time for the funeral and a memorial service the RNLI had organized for the men, which was also attended by the families of the fishermen. The RNLI also put arrangements in place for each family to receive a pension equivalent to that of a Royal Navy petty officer, which would be in addition to any other pensions or state benefits they were due to receive. Further donations for the families were made by the people of Seaham and the surrounding areas.

Following Events

Following the disaster the *George Elmy* was transported to the RNLI's depot in Borehamwood, Hertfordshire where further tests and analysis were carried out. There, just twelve days after the disaster, the batteries were recharged and the engines were successfully restarted, and it was decided that, while the *George Elmy* required extensive repairs, it could be made seaworthy again. Once the repairs were carried out the *George Elmy* was put back into service as an RNLI lifeboat and joined the reserve fleet in Poole Harbour in Dorset where it remained until being decommissioned in 1972.

In the late 1970s, it was announced that the lifeboat station at Seaham would close. The diminishing amount of marine traffic using the harbour due to the declining amount of coal being produced across North East England meant that the station was no longer seen as necessary. A final, symbolic lifeboat launch was carried out on the afternoon of Saturday, 24 February 1979, when *The Will and Fanny Kirby,* the lifeboat which had replaced the *George Elmy*, made its way down the slipway, watched by a crowd of more than 300 people, including representatives of the local council, RNLI and emergency services. The *Will and Fanny Kirby* circled the harbour before heading out to sea, flanked by the lifeboats from Sunderland and Hartlepool as a search and rescue helicopter made a flypast. The ceremony brought 109 years of a RNLI lifeboat being stationed at Seaham to an end. During this time 137 launches had been made and 259 lives saved.

Disappearance, Re-emergence and Return to Seaham

Following its decommissioning from RNLI service at Poole in 1972, the *George Elmy* was sold to a boatyard in Southampton for £600. The *George Elmy* then fell into obscurity as it was sold multiple times to new owners across the UK, none of whom appeared to be aware of the significance or history of the boat they had bought.

In 2009 a member of the East Durham Heritage Group recognised that a fishing boat named the *Miza* which was listed for sale on the e-commerce and auction website eBay was, in fact, the *George Elmy*. Over the years since it left RNLI service it had been renamed multiple times and moved around the country, being based in Great Yarmouth and Grimsby, and was now located in Holyhead, Wales. The East Durham Heritage Group purchased the boat, which was transported to Seaham by road.

The East Durham Heritage Group began raising funds with the aim of carrying out a full restoration of the *George Elmy*, which had declined to a very poor state of repair during its time in private ownership. Donations were sought from companies, charities and the Heritage Lottery Fund with a total of £50,000 eventually being raised. This allowed the restoration to begin at Seaham's North Dock in 2011 before the *George Elmy* was relocated to the River Tyne where Fred Crowell, a traditional boatbuilder, carried out further specialist restoration work.

As the East Durham Heritage Group write of the restoration on the River Tyne:

> Once the boat was sitting securely within its cradle, she was hauled slowly up the slipway into the boathouse which was to be her home for the next two years. The hull was stripped back to reveal the full extent of the ravages of time and the keel was cleaned and de-rusted. Numerous new ribs were crafted and fixed into position whilst rotten and damaged planking was replaced. Two previously acquired diesel engines were ... overhauled in readiness for fitting ... and a milestone was reached with the construction of a new mahogany deck shelter which, when manoeuvred into position, gave the vessel its distinctive lifeboat appearance once again.

On 14 March 2013, the four-year restoration of the *George Elmy* was finally complete and the lifeboat was lowered into the River Tyne. It then sailed to the Marina at Royal Quays under its own power where final adjustments and tests were carried out over the following months. On Sunday, 23 June 2013, fifty-one years after the disaster, the *George Elmy* returned to Seaham Harbour amid a guard of honour provided by RNLI lifeboats from Sunderland, Hartlepool and Tynemouth and a crowd of hundreds of people watched as a blessing and re-naming ceremony took place.

Today the *George Elmy* lifeboat is located in East Durham Heritage and Lifeboat Centre, just yards away from the site of the station where it was based for its time as Seaham's lifeboat. While it no longer goes to sea, the *George Elmy* is on permanent display to the public and is taken out onto the marina for special events. A metre-high stone memorial with the inscription 'Remember the Heroes' and the names of the nine people who lost their lives is also located nearby.

Bibliography

Introduction

Roberts, S E, *Britain's Most Hazardous Occupation: Commercial Fishing*, (Accident Analysis & Prevention, 42 (1): 44 - 49, 2010)

Chapter 1: FV *Gaul*

Bucktin, C, *50 Years on ... Pain of the Gaul Still Runs Deep*, (The Mirror, 9 February 2024)

Dispatches: The Secrets of the Gaul, (Channel 4, Broadcast on 6 November 1997)

Gerrard, J, *Gaul Trawler Tragedy – List of Hull Events to Commemorate 50th Anniversary*, (Hull Daily Mail, 16 January 2024)

Higgens, D, *Judge Asked to Rule on Loss at Sea 30 Years Ago*, (Mirror Group Newspapers, 2004)

Marine Accident Investigation Branch, *Report on the Underwater Survey of the Stern Trawler GAUL H. 243*, (Department of the Environment, Transport and the Regions, London, 1999)

Pallister, D, *MI6 Link to Sunken Trawler Revealed*, (The Guardian, 7 October 2000)

Steel, D, *Report of the Re-opened Formal Investigation into the Loss of the FV Gaul: Part One and Part Two*, The Stationery Office, London, (2004)

West, N, *Historical Dictionary of Naval Intelligence*, (Scarecrow Press, Lanham, 2010)

Chapter 2: The Eyemouth Fishing Disaster

Aitchison, P, (*Black Friday*, Birlinn Limited, Edinburgh, 2001)

Bruce, G, *Wrecks and Reminiscences of St Andrews Bay*, (John Leng & Co, Dundee, 1884)

McPherson, H, *The Scottish Fishing Disaster that Claimed 189 Lives but Which Few Remember*, (The Scotsman, 14 October 2018)

Murray, D S, *Herring Tales: How the Silver Darlings Shaped Human Taste and History* (Bloomsbury Natural History, London, 2016)

Chapter 3: The *Ehime Maru* and USS *Greeneville* Collision

Fein, E, *The Greeneville Submarine Disaster* (Rosen Central, New York, 2002)

Marine Accident Brief, Accident No: DCA-01-MM-022 [*USS Greeneville and Ehime Maru Collision*], (National Transportation Safety Board, Washington DC, 19 October 2005)

Myers, S, L, *Officials Say Captain of Sub Won't Be Tried* (The New York Times, 10 April 2001)

Myers, S L, (2001) *Errors by Submarine Crew Led to Sinking, Court Is Told* (The New York Times, 6 March 2001)

Speakers Group website, page: *Scott Waddle* (viewed at https://www.thespeakersgroup.com/speakers/scott-waddle/ on 26 January 2023)

US Navy Judge Advocate, *Court of Inquiry into the Circumstances Surrounding the Collison of between the USS GREENEVILLE (SSN 772) and Japanese M/V EHIME MARU* (US Naval Corps, 21 April 2001)

Waddle, S and Abraham, K, *The Right Thing* (Integrity Publishing, Brentwood, 2002)

Chapter 4: *Bugaled Breizh*

Allain, P, H, Pierre-*Henri Allain, Shipwreck of the "Bugaled Breizh": a Shipboard on the Run (*Liberation, 19 February 2004) [Translated from French]

BBC News, *French Trawler 'Was Sunk by Sub'* (BBC News website, 24 March 2005, viewed at http://news.bbc.co.uk/1/hi/world/europe/4378899.stm on 19 February 2024)

BBC News, *MoD Clears Sub of Trawler Sinking (*BBC News website, 15 April 2005, viewed at http://news.bbc.co.uk/1/hi/england/cornwall/4447263.stm on 26 February 2024)

BBC News, *Bugaled Breizh: Court of Cassation Closes Trawler Deaths Inquiry* (BBC

BBC News website, 22 June 2016, viewed at https://www.bbc.co.uk/news/uk-england-cornwall-36596311 on 1 March 2024)

BBC News, *Inquiry Into Sunken Boat Re-opens* (BBC News website, 27 November 2009, viewed at http://news.bbc.co.uk/1/hi/england/cornwall/8382962.stm on 23 February 2024)

BBC News, *Bugaled Breizh: Crew Asked Not to Mention Submarine, Inquest Told* (BBC News website, 28 November 2019, viewed at https://www.bbc.co.uk/news/uk-england-cornwall-50591781 on 23 February 2024)

Bureau d'Enquêtes sur les Événements de Mer [BEAMer Report], *Technical Report on the Investigation of the Capsize and Foundering of the Trawler Bugaled Breizh*, (Ministère des Transports, République Française, November 2007)

Chartier, M, *Last Farewell to the "Bugaled Breizh" Before its Deconstruction* (Le Marin, 11 April 2023) [Translated from French]

Gicquel, J, *Bugaled Breizh: Justice Confirms the Dismissal of the Case and Rejects the Families' Appeal*, (20 Minutes, 13 May 2015)

Harrison, D and Finan, T, *MoD 'Covered Up Sinking of French Trawler'* (The Telegraph, 11 February 2007)

Le Monde Reporter, *Bugaled-Breizh: End of Investigation Notified, Additional Investigation Requested (*Le Monde, 4 July 2013) [Translated from French]

Marine Accident Investigation Branch, *Inquest into the Deaths of Yves Marie Gloaguen and Pascal Le Floch Arising from the Loss of the Vessel Bugaled Breizh on 15 January 2004*, UK Government Publication, London, 2021)

Morgan, C, *Bugaled Breizh: Hit and Run on the High Seas?* (Agence Bretagne Presse / Western Morning News, 20 January 2004)

Pike, D, *Disasters at Sea*, (Adlard Coles Nautical / Bloomsbury Publishing, London, 2008)

Samuel, H, *Furious Families of Mystery Shipwreck off Cornwall to Take Case to UK*, (The Telegraph, 15 May 2015)

SOS *Bugaled Breizh* website (viewed at - http://www.bugaledbreizh.org/ on 11 December 2023)

Spotify website, page: *En Eaux Troubles* (viewed at https://open.spotify.com/show/2eC7x0twKGtykT0IaCJwPA on 12 December 2023)

Chapter 5: The *Pelican*

Calvin, T, *Dark Noon: The Final Voyage of the Fishing Boat "Pelican"*, (International Marine/Ragged Mountain Press, Camden, 2005)

Frank Mundus Website (viewed at https://www.fmundus.com/ on 11 October 2023)

McArdle, M, *Making a Living in the Wake of the Pelican Disaster*, (The Atlantic, 28 April 2012)

Moran, K, *The Sinking of Pelican a 'Dark' Tale (*New York Post, 9 September 2005)

United States Coast Guard, *Capsizing of MB Pelican in Vicinity of Montauk Point, Long Island, on 1 September 1951, with Loss of Life*, (Marine Board of Investigation, 8 October 1951)

Chapter 6: The Morecambe Bay Cockling Disaster

BBC News, *Cockling on Sands was 'Madness'*, (BBC News website, 26 September 2005, viewed at http://news.bbc.co.uk/1/hi/england/lancashire/4271642.stm on 12 January 2024)

BBC News, *Cocklers 'Were Warned of Dangers'*, BBC News website, (26 September 2005, viewed at http://news.bbc.co.uk/1/hi/england/lancashire/4284500.stm on 6 January 2024)

BBC News, *Profile of a Gangmaster: Lin Liang Ren*, (BBC News website, 24 March 2006, viewed at http://news.bbc.co.uk/1/hi/world/asia-pacific/4841950.stm on 5 January 2024)

BBC News, *David Morris MP Asks if Cockle Death Trio Were Deported*, (BBC News website, 6 February 2014, viewed at https://www.bbc.co.uk/news/uk-england-lancashire-26046681 on 30 January 2024)

BBC News, *Morecambe Bay cockling Tragedy Victims Remembered 20 Years On*, (BBC News website, 5 February 2024, viewed at https://www.bbc.co.uk/news/uk-england-lancashire-68191697 on 30 January 2024)

Black, S et al (Eds), *Disaster Victim Identification: Experience and Practice*, CRC Press, London, 2011)

Carter, H, Hsiao-Hung, P, and Butt, R, *'Tell the Family to Pray for Me ... I am Dying'*, (The Guardian, 25 March 2005)

Daily Mail Reporter, *Cockler's Jury Hears 999 Call* (The Daily Mail, 21 October 2005)

Goodchild, S, *Dead Cocklers 'Were Being Paid £1 a Day'* (The Independent, 8 February 2004)

Hamer, M, *Rescuers 'Dealing with Unknown'*, (BBC News website, 24 March 2006, viewed at http://news.bbc.co.uk/1/hi/england/4646652.stm on 29 January 2024)

Heinsen, J, Jørgensen, M B and Jørgensen, M O), *Coercive Geographies: Historicizing Mobility, Labor and Confinement*, Brill, Leiden, 2020)

Henriques, R, *From Crime to Crime: Harold Shipman to Operation Midland – 17 Cases That Shocked the World*, Hodder & Stoughton, London, 2020)

Herbert, I, *Gangmaster Guilty of Manslaughter after 21 Chinese Cocklers were Engulfed by Tide* (The Independent, 25 March 2006)

McVeigh, K, *'It's Going to Finish the Village': How Morecambe Bay's Tragedy Changed Cocklepickers' Lives for Ever*, (The Guardian, 4 February 2024)

Press Association, *Cockler Gangmaster Jailed for 14 Years*, (The Guardian, 28 March 2006)

Spencer, R, I Am Up To My Chest In Water. Tell My Family to Pray For Me . . . I Am Dying, (The Telegraph, 11 February 2004).

United Kingdom Maritime Pilots' Association, *Morecambe Bay European Marine Site – Case History*, (Marinebiodiversity.org, 2001)

Westmorland Gazette Reporter, *'Madness' to Open Bay Cockle Beds*, (Westmorland Gazette, 23 September 2005)

Chapter 7: FV *Antares*

Gray, E, *Disasters of the Deep: A Comprehensive Survey of Submarine Accidents and Disasters Paperback* (Pen and Sword Military, Barnsley, 2022)

Hansard [online], HC, *MV Antares*, (Vol 196, Cols 797 – 802, 22 October 1991, viewed at https://hansard.parliament.uk/Commons/1991-10-22/debates/e063537b-29fb-48cd-8142-922d76c342e4/MvAntares, on 23 June 2023)

Harley, N, *Royal Navy Submarine Endangered Lives of Trawlermen after Dragging their Vessel Backwards at High Speed* (The Telegraph, 13 October 2016)

Herald Reporter, *Minister Says No More Action on Antares Sinking*, (The Herald, 20 October 1992)

Lavery, B, *Shield of Empire: The Royal Navy and Scotland*, (Birlinn Limited, Edinburgh, 2012)

Marine Accident Investigation Branch, *Report of the Chief Inspector of Marine Accidents into the Collision Between the Fishing Vessel Antares and HMS Trenchant*, (HMSO, London, 1992)

Marine Accident Investigation Branch, *Collision Between the Stern Trawler Karen and a Dived Royal Navy Submarine*, (HMSO, London, 2016)

Royle, T, *Facing the Bear: Scotland and the Cold War*, (Birlinn Limited, Edinburgh, 2019)

Chapter 8: *Solway Harvester*

Allison, A, *Three Fishermen Saved as Solway Sister Ship Sinks*, (The Guardian, 15 August 2000)

BBC News, *Politicians Criticised Over Harvester Salvage*, (BBC News website, 13 February 2000, viewed at http://news.bbc.co.uk/1/hi/scotland/641525.stm on 12 April 2024)

BBC News, *Harvester Sister Boats Detained*, BBC News website (28 February 2000, viewed at http://news.bbc.co.uk/1/hi/scotland/659411.stm on 15 April 2024)

BBC News, *Solway Harvester Trial Collapses*, BBC News website (18 May 2005, viewed at http://news.bbc.co.uk/1/hi/scotland/4559393.stm on 29 March 2024)

BBC News, *Solway Judge Outlines His Reasons* (BBC News website, 18 May 2005, viewed at http://news.bbc.co.uk/1/hi/scotland/4559931.stm on 11 March 2024)

BBC News, *Scrapping Brings End to 'Macabre' Solway Harvester Site* (BBC News website, 11 November 2013, viewed at https://www.bbc.co.uk/news/world-europe-isle-of-man-24901224 on 1 March 2024)

BBC News, *Curtain to Fall on Solway Harvester After Storm Delays* (BBC News website, 15 January 2014, viewed at https://www.bbc.co.uk/news/world-europe-isle-of-man-25743715 on 23 April 2024)

Brocklebank, J, *Family of Drowned Fisherman Will Never See £500k Damages,* (Scottish Daily Mail, 27 August 2015)

Daily Record Reporter, *Did Nuclear Sub Sink the Harvester?; Families Told of Damage to Fishing Boat's Hull*, (The Daily Record, 22 January 2000)

Fishing Vessels (Safety Provisions) Rules 1975, (UK Statutory Instruments 1975 No 330, Merchant Shipping Safety, 1975)

Herald Reporter, *Boat Owner in Court Five Years after Solway Harvester Sank Charges Against Co-accused Dropped*, (The Herald, 12 April 2005)

Herald Reporter, *Inquiry into Boat Sinking Claims*, (The Herald, 6 November 2000)

Marine Accident Investigation Branch, *Investigation of the Capsize and Sinking of the Fishing Vessel Solway Harvester BA794 11 Miles East of the Isle of Man on 11 January 2000 with the Loss of 7 Lives*, (Report No 1/2006, MAIB, February 2006)

Marine Accident Investigation Branch, *Foundering, 11 Miles to the East of the Isle of Man FV Solway Harvester with the Loss of Seven Lives on 11 January 2000*, (MAIB

Marine Accident Investigation Branch, *Report on the Investigation of the Loss of a Crewman from the Fishing Vessel St, Amant (BA 101) off the Coast of North-west Wales on 13 January 2012*, (Accident Report, Report No 1/2013, January 2013)

Press Association, *Solway Harvester Owner Cleared of Manslaughter* (The Guardian, 18 May 2005)

Press Association, *Solway Harvester Crew Deaths Were Accidental, Says Coroner*, (The Guardian, 8 November 2008)

Safety Bulletin 1/2000, DETR Environment Transport Regions, February 2000)

Seenan, G, *Families Dismayed as Trial of Trawler Owner Collapses* (The Guardian, 19 May 2005)

Williams, M, *No Criminal Negligence in Dredger Death, Says Coroner*, (The Herald, 19 April 2013)

Chapter 9: The 1914 Newfoundland Sealing Disasters

Bailey, S, *Canada Loses WTO Appeal: EU Seal Products Ban Upheld*, (CTV News website, 22 May 2014)

Baker, M, *The Struggle for Influence and Power: William Coaker, Abram Kean, and the Newfoundland Sealing Industry 1908-1915*, (Newfoundland and Labrador Studies, 28 (1))

Brown, C, and Horwood, H, *Death On The Ice: The Great Newfoundland Sealing Disaster Of 1914*, (Doubleday, New York, 1972)

CBC, *This Doomed Ship Saved Newfoundlanders – And Defended Russians – Before Its Demise 80 Years Ago*, (Canadian Broadcasting Corporation website, 29 December, 2021, viewed at https://www.cbc.ca/news/canada/newfoundland-labrador/bellaventure-remembered-1.6283555 on 1 May 2024)

Colman, J S, *The Newfoundland Seal Fishery and the Second World War*, (Journal of Animal Ecology, 18 (1): 40-46, 1949)

Cooke, R, *Seal Hunt Advocate Takes Issue with EU President's Claim that Indigenous Exemptions are Working*, (Canadian Broadcasting Corporation website, 24 November 2023, viewed at https://www.cbc.ca/news/canada/newfoundland-labrador/seal-hunt-exemption-1.7039447 on 23 March 2024)

Fink, S, *2022 Commercial Seal Hunt in Canada: A Spring of Sorrows or Sustainable Solutions?* (viewed at https://www.ifaw.org/uk/journal/commercial-seal-hunt-canada-2022 on 20 February 2024)

Heritage Newfoundland and Labrador website, page: *Conducting the 19th Century Seal Fishery*, (viewed at https://www.heritage.nf.ca/articles/economy/19-century-seal.php on 1 February 2024)

Higgins, J, *Perished: The 1914 Newfoundland Seal Hunt Disaster*, (Boulder Publications, 2014)

Horwood, W, Emerson, J, *Report of the Commission of Enquiry into the Sealing Disasters of 1914*, (The Government of Newfoundland and Labrador, 27 February 2015)

Kean, A, *Old and Young Ahead: A Millionaire in Seals*, Heath Cranton, London, 1935)

Ryan, S, *The Ice Hunters: A History of Newfoundland Sealing to 1914*, Breakwater Books Ltd, St Johns, 2012)

Wrecksite website, page: *SS Alexander Sibiriakov*, (viewed at https://www.wrecksite.eu/wreck.aspx?58649 on 6 February 2024)

Chapter 10: FV *Destination*

Bernton, H, *Overloading, Heavy Ice and an Open Hatch: Coast Guard Details What Sank the Seattle-based Destination* (Seattle Times, 10 February 2019)

Bernton, H, and Bush, E, *Overloading, Heavy Ice and an Open Hatch: Coast Guard Details what Sank the Seattle-based Destination*, (Seattle Times, 3 March 2019)

Dew, C, 2010, *Historical Perspective on Habitat Essential to Bristol Bay Red King Crab* in Kruse, G H, et al (Eds), *Biology and Management of Exploited Crab Populations Under Climate Change* (Alaska Sea Grant, University of Alaska, Fairbanks, 2010)

Hill, S, *NOAA Ships Locate Wreck of F/V Destination*, (National Fisherman, 24 July 2004)

National Institute for Occupational Safety & Health / NIOSH, *Fatalities in the Commercial Fishing Industry*, 28 April 1999)

Sullivan, T, Kodiak Daily Mirror, *The Early Years of the Kodiak King Crab Fishery*, 14 October 2014)

United States Coast Guard, *Marine Board Investigation Commercial Fishing Vessel Destination Casualty – Formal Hearing*, (Henry M Jackson Federal Building, Seattle, Washington, 7 August -17 August, 2017)

United States Coast Guard, *Report of the Marine Board of Investigation into the Commercial Fishing Vessel Destination Sinking and Loss of the Vessel With all Six Crewmembers Missing and Presumed Deceased Approximately 4.4 NM Northwest of St George Island, Alaska on February 11, 2017*, (US Department of Homeland Security, 27 February 2019)

Chapter 11: José Salvador Alvarenga

Agence France-Presse, *How Castaway Jose Salvador Alvarenga Survived 18 Months at Sea*, (NDTV website, 16 February 2014, viewed at https://www.ndtv.com/world-news/how-castaway-jose-salvador-alvarenga-survived-18-months-at-sea-550947 on 22 April 2024)

Dellaverson, C, Smith, A and Bruton, B, *Castaway's Parents Thought They Would Never See Son Again* (NBC News, 4 February 2014)

Gardner, D, *Castaway Who Survived 13 Months Adrift on Pacific Ocean Has Lie Detector and Medical Test 'Proof' He Is Not a Fake* (Daily Mail, 3 April 2014)

Haddou, L, *Pacific Castaway Recounts His 13-month Odyssey* (The Guardian, 3 February 2014)

Franklin, J, *438 Days: An Extraordinary True Story of Survival at Sea* (Macmillan, London)

Jones, D, *Castaway Who Survived 14 Months Adrift on the Pacific Angrily Denies He Ate His Dead Companion* (Daily Mail, 24 April 2014)

Lah, K, *Real-life Castaway Survived 438 Days Lost at Sea*, (CNN website, 10 January, 2016, viewed at https://edition.cnn.com/2016/01/08/world/rewind-real-life-castaway/index.html on 3 April 2024)

Osbourne, S, *Salvador Alvarenga: Castaway Who Survived 15 Months at Sea Sued For $1m After Being Accused of 'Eating Colleague'* (The Independent, 15 December 2015)

Payne, W, *Why Pacific Castaway Left wife and Child Behind: Jose Alvarenga Fled El Salvador for Mexico After Bar room Brawl Left Him Fighting for His Life* (Daily Mail, 6 February 2014)

Pearlman, J, *Too Incredible To Be True? Survivor Tells of Pacific Ordeal* (The Telegraph, 3 February 2014)

Withnall, A, *Castaway Jose Salvador Alvarenga's 'Incredible Story': Official Says Fishy Tale May Be Too Good To Be True* (The Independent, 4 February 2014)

Chapter 12: The Seaham Lifeboat Disaster

BBC News, *George Elmy Lifeboat Returns to Seaham After 51 Years* (BBC News website, 24 June 2013, viewed at https://www.bbc.co.uk/news/uk-england-tyne-23026788 on 15 May 2024)

BIBLIOGRAPHY

Chrystal, P, *Lifeboat Stations of North East England From Sunderland to the Humber Through Time* (Amberley Publishing, Stroud, 2012)

Cooper, E, Maitland, G and Scollen, B, *George Elmy Lifeboat* (Seaham. gov.uk website)

Davies, J (Ed.), *Seaham Station Closes*, (The Life-boat: Journal of the RNLI, 46 (467): 127 - 128, 1972)

Devlin, J, *The Seaham Lifeboat Disaster* (The Police Journal: Theory, Practice and Principles, 41 (5): 199 - 204, 1963)

Doe, H, *One Crew: The RNLI's Official 200-Year History,* (Amberley Publishing, Stroud, 2024)

East Durham Heritage and Lifeboat Centre, *Seaham Lifeboat Disaster*, East Durham Heritage Group Website

Hansard [online], HC, *Seaham Harbour Lifeboat (Loss)* (Vol 667, Cols 1010 - 1012, 20 November 1962, viewed at https://api.parliament.uk/historic-hansard/commons/1962/nov/20/seaham-harbour-lifeboat-loss on 10 May 2024)

National Historic Ships UK, *George Elmy* (National Historic Ships UK website)

Seaham Town Council, *Post War Redevelopment 1945 - 1993*, Seaham. gov.uk website)

The Life-Boat Journal, *The Seaham Disaster* (The Life-boat: Journal of the RNLI, 37: 403): 406 – 409, 1963)